What The Professionals Are Saying About
WIN ALL DAY - FOR ATHLETES

"This is a must read for athletes, coaches and anyone who wants to win in life! As a Pro-Bowler and Super Bowl Champion in the NFL I understand the importance of mental focus and preparation. To now have a simple step by step 27 day gameplan for athletes is awesome! Coach JC will motivate you and inspire you to think bigger and Create The Winning Mindset so that you can achieve peak performance on and off the field. If you are ready to win as a coach or an athlete then you need to read, WIN ALL DAY - FOR ATHLETES from my friend Coach JC."

- Joe Theismann
   Super Bowl Champion

"If you're an athlete and want to achieve more, read and absorb the strategies in this brilliant book by my friend Coach JC!"

- James Malinchak
   Featured on ABC's Hit TV Show, "Secret Millionaire"
   Founder, www.BigMoneySpeaker.com

"After reading Jonathan Conneely's book "WIN ALL DAY - FOR ATHLETES" my first reaction was that this is something all of us should read no matter what our age or career. The important reminders for those of us that are in our careers are worth the time and effort investing in this book and Coach JC's principles.

And for the athletes I can simply say this: Jonathan's emphasis on the concept of "mindset" is critical to success in the world of athletics as well as the world you will enter once the game says it's time. If you take the 27 principles that Jonathan lays out and make them a part of your everyday life you will definitely become the best "you" that you can become. And that is the challenge of sports and life. To reach "your" best level!

I encourage you to read this book a number of times so that you can fully understand the "what"; the "why"; and the "how" of becoming successful in your athletic career and your life. What Jonathan lays out is "the truth"!"

– Kevin Eastman

Assistant Coach Los Angeles Clippers
2008 NBA World Champion Coach with the Boston Celtics
2008 & 2010 NBA All Star Game Coach with the Boston Celtics

"As a professional athlete, I understand what it takes to get to the top, because I have lived it! Coach JC's book is a must read for everyone. If you have a goal to attain, in the athletic realm or in life, this book is for you! Read this book, implement Coach JC's teaching, and watch your world transform!"

– *Johnny Quinn*

U.S. National Bobsled Team Member, Former NFL Athlete (Buffalo Bills, Green Bay Packers); CEO & Founder of The Athlete Watch, a pro-active leadership course in college recruiting; www.TheAthleteWatch.com

---

"JC is a fantastic trainer, teacher, speaker and life success coach. I've heard and read many "experts" speak about the mental approach of life and sports, but I have never seen someone present these concepts and techniques in such a practical and insightful way. This is a must read for all athletes looking to take there game to a higher level."

– *Ian Rubel*

Senior Vice President at Pinnacle Management Corp.

"Coach JC is not only a world class coach, presenter and author, he's a world class human being, period. This book gives you JC's world class coaching and advice 24/7 at your fingertips. High performance requires coaching and it all starts with mindset. Get this book!"

– *Alwyn and Rachel Cosgrove*

Owner Results Fitness

"Coach JC has nailed it in this book! His passion for motivating people to achieve their dreams and a clear-cut path to get there has come together in WIN ALL DAY - FOR ATHLETES. Coach JC lays out a clear and detailed plan for athletes young and old to achieve success both in the arena and in the game of LIFE!"

– Dave Owens
Former Collegiate Football Player & Member of the US Bobsled Team, Creator of The Hand Speed Trainer

---

"This book, I can say is a SHORTCUT for all the secrets of mindset that ALL athletes must know. Thanks Coach JC!"

– Fabio Leopoldo
3X World Jiu Jitsu Champion IFL Team MMA Champion - Renzo Gracie Team Head Instructor Gracie Morumbi MMA/BJJ Team

---

"This is a must read for athletes, coaches, or anyone who aspires to achieve the ultimate in what they want to accomplish. Coach JC clearly identifies the concept that Peak Performance occurs only when the mind and body are working in unison to maximize your full potential."

– Bill Springman
Minnesota Twins, Minor League Hitting Coordinator

"Through working with at risk youth, WBO uses baseball to train the mindset of youth to overcome whatever struggles and obstacles they may have in life. Focusing on faith as a cornerstone of this mindset also gives youth a foundation to apply to all areas of life even without sports. JC through this book has helped me discover The Secret To Real Athlete Success and how it is a perfect read to help me inspire youth to continue with athletics and for those who want to continue to win in all areas of life."

– Jerry Jacobson
Creator World Baseball Outreach

"Jonathan Conneely is one of the most positive and motivated people I have ever met. His drive to be successful is infectious and his ability to connect and encourage others to get the most out of their gifts is unparalleled. He is committed to excellence in all aspects of his life, and I am blessed to call him a friend and mentor."

– Kyle Wills
Athletic Director at Cornerstone Christian Schools

Win All Day - For Athletes
Copyright © 2020 by Jonathan Conneely

Published by:
JJC Enterprises
8177 S Harvard Ave.
Suite 420
Tulsa, OK 74137

All rights reserved. No part of this book may be reproduced or transmitted in any form or by any means, electronic or mechanical, including photocopying, recording or by any information storage and retrieval system without written permission of the publisher except for brief quotations used in reviews, written specifically for inclusion in a newspaper or magazine.

Warning- Disclaimer

The purpose of this book is to educate and entertain. The author or publisher does not guarantee that anyone following the ideas, tips, suggestions, techniques or strategies will become successful. The author and publisher shall assume no liability or responsibility to anyone with respect to any loss or damage caused, or alleged to be caused, directly or indirectly, by the information contained in the book.

Cover and Layout Design by aspiretodesign.com

ISBN: 978-0-578-79903-2

Printed in the United Stated of America

www.CoachJC.com

HOW TO CREATE THE WINNING MINDSET TO WIN AS AN ATHLETE AND WIN IN LIFE!

Coach JC
Johnathan Conneely
WWW.COACHJC.COM

A SPECIAL THANK YOU TO MY TEAM

For God

My Lord and Savior,

I would not be who I am today if it weren't for Him

For Jodi, my Beautiful Wife

My Love and Inspiration

For my Mom, the best coach I have ever met.

For my Dad, you're an over comer and an inspiration.

For my Sis, Jaime, thanks for always believing in me.

For my daughter, Alivia, you are my sunshine.

For The WIN ALL DAY Family

and all the dedicated athletes

I have been blessed to work with.

CONTENTS

Chapter 1: GET WHAT YOU CAME FOR 13
Chapter 2: WHAT'S MY WHY? 17
Chapter 3: KNOWLEDGE IS POWER 21
Chapter 4: WHAT'S MY GAME PLAN? 25
Chapter 5: TAKE MASSIVE ACTION 29
Chapter 6: I DON'T ACCEPT FAILURE 33
Chapter 7: NO MORE EXCUSES 37
Chapter 8: LET NEGATIVITY GO 41
Chapter 9: CHECK YOURSELF 45
Chapter 10: CHANGE YOUR THINKING 49
Chapter 11: WHAT AM I REALLY AFRAID OF? 53
Chapter 12: LIVE, LEARN & MOVE ON, BABY! 57
Chapter 13: NO QUIT 61
Chapter 14: THINK BIGGER 65
Chapter 15: AM I ACCOUNTABLE? 69
Chapter 16: DO YOU FEEL IT? 73
Chapter 17: GET BACK IN THE RACE 77
Chapter 18: ALL DAY! 81
Chapter 19: SEPARATE YOURSELF! 85
Chapter 20: BE A CONTROL FREAK 89
Chapter 21: TAKE THE LID OFF! 93
Chapter 22: HOW'S MY AGILITY? 97
Chapter 23: DETERMINE YOUR PRIORITIES 101
Chapter 24: SET YOUR GOALS 105
Chapter 25: DECIDE TO SPEAK IT 109
Chapter 26: DIG DEEP 115
Chapter 27: JUST DO IT 119

ABOUT JONATHAN CONNEELY

COACH JC

Coach JC coaches people on a daily basis on How to Create the Winning Mindset and WIN!

AS A LIFESTYLE, FITNESS AND STRENGTH COACH, COACH JC'S NO NONSENSE, NO EXCUSE APPROACH HAS BEEN TRANSFORMING LIVES FOR OVER 17 YEARS NOW.

As an established Author, Speaker, and Coach he is regarded as one of the top Coaches in the entire country. He has been blessed to assist athletes in "Creating the Winning Mindset" so that they can WIN and Take It to the Next level! Coach JC has motivated and personally coached athletes from nine years of age to some of the top athletes in the world. Coach JC has a passion for helping people live the life they were born to live.

He is the creator of the WIN ALL DAY Academy and the founder of the well recognized Sports Performance Company: Dynamic Sports Development.

In addition, Coach JC was the Director of Strength and Conditioning at an NCAA Division I Institution for 10 years. Coach JC's coaching philosophy remains consistent in that he is dedicated to providing the tools necessary to empower athletes to create the Focus, Discipline, and Confidence needed to achieve GREAT Success in life and WIN every day.

Coach JC's qualifications include a Bachelors of Science degree, a Life Coach certification, a Sports Psychology Coach, multiple coaching, sports performance, and fitness certifications, with none more valuable than his 12 years in the trenches – training over 5,000 athletes at all levels.

He is the author of the WIN ALL DAY book series. He has also been a trainer and coach to professional athletes, corporations, pageant contestants, businessmen, entrepreneurs, pastors, and others just like you.

IF YOU WOULD LIKE TO LEARN MORE ABOUT COACH JC, PLEASE VISIT

www.CoachJC.com

Coach JC is available for speaking engagements, life success coaching, radio and television interviews, and much more.

PLEASE CONTACT US TO MAKE COACH JC A PART OF YOUR LIFE!

1-800-382-1506

jc@coachjc.com

A FEW WORDS OF INSPIRATION FROM THE AUTHOR & CREATOR

COACH JC!

Congratulations! *You are about to separate yourself as an athlete! I absolutely LOVE helping athletes just like you in preparing both physically and mentally so that you can set yourself up to achieve great success in sport and life. I realized through my own life and in coaching athletes for over 17 years that most athletes have big dreams, goals, and ambitions and are just one step away from making those dreams, goals, and ambitions a reality. Having a dream is usually not the problem; the problem is having the RIGHT game plan and executing the essential action steps to make those dreams a reality.*

> "IF YOU WANT SOMETHING YOU'VE NEVER HAD, YOU'VE GOT TO DO SOMETHING YOU'VE NEVER DONE
>
> ..AND DO IT EVERY DAY!"

Success or failure is not just some big event that happens one day.

Michael Jordan did not just wake up one day as the greatest basketball player ever.

Dylan Bundy did not just become the top pitching prospect in MLB right out of high school by chance.

Alex Rodriguez was not projected as the greatest baseball player ever to now being labeled as a player who chokes in the postseason.

Tiger Woods did not go from being projected as the greatest golfer ever to become a fallen star by accident.

WINNING or losing are about the things or lack of things that YOU DECIDE to do or not do day-in and day-out.

WINNING IN ATHLETICS OR IN LIFE IS SIMPLE...

It takes ONLY two things!

1. You MUST Create the Winning Mindset so that you can unlock your full potential as an athlete and become dominate in your sport and in life!
2. You MUST have the RIGHT game plan and you MUST execute the RIGHT daily action steps of that game plan every single day.

This book will provide you with the RIGHT 27-day game plan so that you can achieve greatness in your athletic career and in life. I will coach you on how to unlock the power of your mind so that you can WIN each and every day and get what you desire as an athlete.

You can now play at the next level, start dominating, and become a successful athlete. You can now stop wishing and hoping but rather have a certainty that you WILL succeed. How do I know? Because I did exactly that! Utilizing the same 27-day game plan that you have right here, I was able to pull myself out of a deep personal tragedy and create lasting success in my life.

With this same game plan, I was able to land my first job as the Director of Strength & Conditioning at the NCAA Division I level before I even graduated from college.

With this same game plan, I was able to open my dream sports performance facility, Dynamic Sports Development, and over the last 12 years have been fortunate and blessed to train some of the top athletes in the entire world.

By implementing this same game plan at the age of 29, I was named Tulsa's Young Entrepreneur of the Year, was selected as one of Oklahoma's 30 under 30 Entrepreneurs, and was also selected as one of Oklahoma's 40 under 40 Entrepreneurs.

With this same game plan, I have been able to assist athletes of all levels achieve greatness in their respective sports and in life.

IS THIS LUCK? HECK NO!

I tell you this because if I – an Italian kid from the Jersey shore with no success background –can do it, then you can too!

If this same game plan has helped thousands of athletes achieve greatness in their sports and in their lives, then it will work for you as well!

This book is short, simple, and everything you need to WIN as an athlete and in life. This game plan will not work for you unless you work it. This one book has the potential to absolutely Take Your Game to the Next Level and set you up to WIN.

ARE YOU READY?

If so, then I have just one more question for you...

If you want something you've never had, you've got to....

WIN ALL DAY WAY

The WIN ALL DAY WAY is what it takes to become a great athlete and is our pyramid of building a WINNING athlete: "YOU." You must train all three components the RIGHT way each and every day. Just like you train your body, you MUST train your mind. To WIN ALL DAY as an athlete is a mindset...Creating The Winning Mindset is The Secret and is the differentiator in becoming a GREAT athlete.

ARE YOU WINNING?

You see, most athletes believe that winning takes place during the actual competition or event itself. While you do have to perform in order to win, winning actually comes down to what you have been doing leading up to the performance or competition.

Winning is a choice and you make that choice each and every day in order to become a great athlete.

On the previous page I gave you my proven system that has produced some of the top athletes in the World: THE WIN ALL DAY WAY. You have three components that you must execute each and every day to be great as an athlete.

Now the key is EACH AND EVERY DAY. To WIN you must do what needs to be done each and every day, period. You MUST WIN each and every day!

I have been training athletes for over 12 years now and throughout my career, I have seen the athlete who had all the talent in the world, go on and never achieve ultimate success. I have also seen the kid who most people thought would never make it, go on to achieve great success in his respective sport. Why is this? Well, I truly believe that over the last 12 years of coaching, I have figured out the secret. Most athletes are not winning every day and most athletes don't believe they can win every day. Winning is a mindset and that is why I created my Create the Winning Mindset System. I truly believe that you can have anything you want once you create the winning mindset.

Most athletes don't know that just like you train your body, you can train your mind. So in this book I will reveal to you "Your 27-Day Game Plan on How to Create the Winning Mindset and WIN Every Day as an Athlete and in Life."

I will provide you with my proven system on how to train your mind so that you can become a mental giant and have the focus you want, the discipline you desire, and the confidence you need to take the right action to win every day.

WHO IS THIS GAME PLAN FOR?

I have used this game plan effectively with athletes, parents, and coaches so if you are...

*The Athlete who wants to be GREAT

*The Parent who wants to assist your child in being GREAT

*The Coach who wants his team to be GREAT

Then this game plan is for you!

HOW DOES THE GAME PLAN WORK?

The "Create the Winning Mindset" game plan consists of 27 principles.

You will use these principles to train your mind just like you train your body.

I have found three ways that you can effectively implement the 27 principles of the "Creating the Wining Mindset" system and I encourage you to pick which one will work best for you.

1. You can execute one principle every day for 27 consecutive days.
2. You can execute two principles a week and make it a 13-week game plan.
3. You can make it a 27-week game plan and space it out by implementing just one principle each week.

Many coaches have utilized this third technique and have been very successful with their teams. Each week, the coach emphasizes one principle to his athletes, and then he has his athletes implement the Winning Action Steps until they have mastered them.

The goal for you is to execute the game plan and adopt these principles as part of who you are as an athlete. So no matter how you choose to complete the game plan, you never stop using the principles. These are principles that you will continue to execute, refine, and utilize in your journey to success. This book was created as a game plan that you can keep with you at all times. You will use it just like any other training tool to continue to grow and achieve greatness as an athlete and in life.

THE KEY TO YOUR SUCCESS:

For you to Create the Winning Mindset, you must not just read the principles; you must put them into action. Retention without implementation is useless, my friend. Make sure to take each Winning Action Step for the day and WIN at it in all you do. Find ways to put it into action in your personal and professional life. You want to develop the right motor patterns and habits now so that it is part of your subconscious mind and you can pull on it when needed.

The Daily Action Steps must be a part of your training! Just like you train your body day-in and day-out, you now have the right game plan to train your mind, Create the Wining Mindset and WIN as an athlete each day. With each principle you will be given your Daily Action Step; by answering the questions honestly with yourself and taking massive action each day, you will WIN.

The Winning Confession is your time to speak it! You will see that each day or with each principle you have a Winning Confession. Faith comes by hearing, and this is your time to speak those things that you desire into your life. It is during this time that you call those things that are not into existence. Some people have used this practice – known as positive affirmations – successfully. Your Winning Confession is a lot more than just speaking positive stuff each day. It's about you starting to THINK, ACT, and FEEL as if you're already there! You will learn more about the power of your Winning Confession and how to confess it later in the book. You need to do two things immediately when it comes to your Winning Confession:

YOU NEED TO SEE IT AND SAY IT!

You will say it like you mean it – out loud – at least two times a day. This is powerful as it will pull you to build up your faith and help you to find creative ways to make it happen.

You will see at the end of each principle that I provide you with a real-life story from an athlete or coach who has achieved WINNING by utilizing this same system that you have right now. I show you these for one reason only: to motivate you and inspire you to know that if it worked for them it will also work for you. You just have to work it just like they did!

I like to win and the fact that you have picked up this book at this time in your life tells me you also like to win. We all want to win. Most every athlete I speak with wants to be successful. However, the ones who actually win are those that change the wanting, wishing, and hoping to making the necessary sacrifices that it takes to WIN!

So before you start this game plan, I want you to ask yourself a question, "Am I willing to commit to execute this game plan and do what it takes to Create the Winning Mindset?"

IF YOU ARE ABLE, WILLING, AND READY, THEN LET'S ROLL!

CHAPTER ONE

GET WHAT YOU CAME FOR

"To get what you want in life you must first make a very important choice...you must decide what it is you want!"

– Coach JC

WHAT IS IT THAT YOU REALLY WANT?

If you don't know what you want, you will never get it! It all starts right here, my friend. It all starts with desire! You Must Want It! You must have a desire to achieve and a desire to succeed!

Get What You Came For! This is a line that my athletes hear from me all the time. I remind them constantly to "Get What You Came For." For you to get what you came for, you have got to know what it is you came for.

So, what is that thing that you may have wished for or hoped for – that thing that you may have been dreaming about since you were a kid? Maybe it's to make the varsity squad, earn that college scholarship, be an All-American, get drafted into the Pros, be an All-Star, or maybe even be selected into the Hall of Fame.

If you don't know what it is, you'll never get it! This is the big picture, the thing you dream of, your ultimate goal. What does that look like to you? We all have those things that we want to get or achieve, but so many times it's just about refining it to know EXACTLY what it is. You have to be specific about it. You have to be vivid about it. If you don't know where you want to go, you'll never get there. This is so important because WHAT YOU DESIRE IS WHERE YOUR FOCUS WILL

GO! Once you know what it is that you desire, you must then place a timeline on it. When will you accomplish this desire by?

WINNING starts with DESIRE! Most athletes are afraid to put their "What" out there because they don't want to set themselves up for failure. It is your "What" that will determine where you put your focus and the minute you decide to focus on something is the moment when you give it meaning in life. That meaning will produce the necessary emotions that create the action to get you your "What".

Your "What" is what will start to drive you in Creating the Winning Mindset as an athlete.

You have got to be real about it, be specific about it, and put it out there. Michael Jordan was never unclear about his "What". His response was always the same in that he played to be the greatest player to ever play the game.

So today, to Create the Winning Mindset you will define your "What".

WINNING ACTION!

Be Specific. Be Vivid. Have a Timeline.

What is it that I really want?

_____

_____

How much do I really desire this?

_____

_____

When do I desire this by?

_____

_____

WINNING CONFESSION!

I WILL Create the Winning Mindset and WIN as an ATHLETE and in LIFE. I WILL achieve my greatest potential as an athlete and I WILL succeed in LIFE! I am a WINNER!

A WINNING ATHLETE...

"Mindset is EVERYTHING! "As a man thinketh so is he". How you think is who you will become and how you will perform. Most importantly it will dictate how you will live your life. By the grace of God I've been blessed with the opportunity to be showered by Coach JC with moral, physical and most importantly spiritual knowledge. He has helped transform my mindset into one of a Champion, man of God and world changer, which is critical for one to succeed.

When I think back at every conversation we have had, two words come to mind, "Separate Yourself." God only created one version of you for a reason and when you can embrace that fully you become an original on the market instead of somebody else's knock-off. That mindset is what it takes to pursue your dreams, transform your thoughts into positive ones and be successful in whatever it is you set your heart on. If I think like a Champion, then nothing can stop me. If i think like a man of God, then I do what's right even when no one is looking. If I think like a WORLD changer, then I WILL shake this nation. It all starts with a right mindset and ends with crooked thinking. Coach JC has given you the keys in this book, now it's your job to unlock and unleash the power."

– Moses Ehambe, Professional Basketball Athlete

CHAPTER TWO

WHAT'S MY WHY?

"You must have dreams and goals if you are ever going to achieve anything in this world."

– Lou Holtz

NOW THAT YOU HAVE DEFINED YOUR "WHAT" YOU NEED TO NOW ASK YOURSELF, "WHY?"

When I'm coaching an athlete, immediately after discovering his "What" my next question is always, "Why?" Why do you want to play in the NFL or the NBA or whatever it is he stated as his goal.

I remember it like it was yesterday. I asked this exact question to an athlete that told me he wanted to get drafted to play Major League Baseball. His response, "For all of my life I have watched my mom work many jobs, two and even three, so that she could support me and my brother. It has always been my dream to play MLB, but I need to get drafted so that I can pay off my mom's house and car and provide her with an opportunity to only work if she wants to."

Man! Is that not a powerful "Why"? This kid had a purpose, a burning desire of why he wanted to accomplish his goal. I get goose bumps thinking about it.

I am excited to say that we turned his want into an "I WILL," and he was drafted and able to help his mom financially!

Why do you want that thing that you want? Determining your "Why" is absolutely crucial for you as an athlete to take it to the next level. Your "Why" is your purpose: the burning desire of why you have to have the "What". It is the reason that you will do what you do day-in and day-out to reach ultimate success in athletics.

Your purpose is what will drive you. It will keep you motivated, and it is what is going to make your dream a reality. This is your burning passion to make that desire, your "What" a reality. This is the reason for why you do what you do, the thing that you will stay focused on: The End Result!

For you to truly WIN, you must know your reason why. What makes you tick? This is more than your goals; it's your need, your target. It's that thing that pulls on you so strong; it's so attractive that you have got to have it.

I want you to hear me here; your follow through in executing your daily action steps comes down to your emotional state of intensity and this is why your vision has got to be compelling enough to drive you. When your "Why" is strong your emotional intensity is strong. Every action you take originates with a thought and once your emotional intensity is on point each and every action you take will have to line up with that level. You see it?

You will Create the Winning Mindset today by defining your "Why". **Knowing your purpose is a MUST!**

WINNING ACTION!

Be Specific. Be Vivid.

Why do I really want this?

_____

_____

How bad do I want/need this?

_____

_____

What am I willing to do to get it?

_____

_____

What am I not willing to do?

_____

_____

WINNING CONFESSION!

I have been created with a purpose! I am not moved by what I feel or circumstances that happen. I WILL take purposeful action to get what I desire. I Will Create The Winning Mindset! I am a WINNER!

A WINNING ATHLETE...

"Coach JC's 27 day game plan gives you a step by step process on how to go from developing your mind, to then turning that into action and applying it to the physical. You can't have one without the other! Alot of my success that I have achieved over the years on the basketball court has been due to a great deal of what Coach JC has taught me and challenged me to accomplish. "The Secret to Real Athlete Success" is an amazing book that will empower athletes on all level's on how to push through adversity and "Create The Winning Mindset"!

"Coach JC, is the best at what he does. His passion and knowledge helped me grow into the athlete I am today. Seeing his enthusiasm just made me want to work that much harder! He took an average joe and made him into a pro" My highschool coach always said, "I believe you win with average people doing above average things" And that's what you do with Coach JC, above average things!"

– *Yemi Ogunoye, Professional Basketball Athlete*

CHAPTER THREE

KNOWLEDGE IS POWER

"Perfection is not attainable, but if we chase perfection we can catch excellence."

– Vince Lombardi

YOU'VE HEARD IT BEFORE...

People perish for the lack of knowledge! I say it a little differently: "people perish for the lack of the RIGHT Knowledge!" With so much information out there it's easy to get overwhelmed and overloaded. I want you to focus now on what you really need to know to get what you want. What do you need to do today to get the RIGHT information, to gain the RIGHT knowledge, to get what you truly desire? You will always be a student and constantly be learning, but starting today, you will stay focused on the RIGHT information. Forget about everything else, my friend; knowledge is power, and today you will discover the RIGHT knowledge!

What is it that you need in order to perfect your skill at your sport? What kind of training must you participate in to get to the level you want? Knowledge is power, and now you can have the peace of mind that when it comes to your training, you have the RIGHT game plan to Create the Winning Mindset.

You have to gain a respect for this knowledge. Your job is to be a great athlete, and once you begin to feel that your present job is important, you will become enthusiastic about being GREAT.

Before you ever make it to the next level, you have to maximize the moment and start to take pride in where you are currently. A direct correlation exists between how you feel about your job and how you perform. Your job right now is to be the BEST you can be at the moment. Your job is to gather all the RIGHT information and knowledge you need to be successful as an athlete right now.

Many times we get so concerned with the future and where we want to be that we aren't who we fully need to be in the present. Start to be the greatest student of your sport now. Start now to become the hardest worker at your current level. Start to develop the discipline and enthusiasm now so that you can create the right habits to become a great athlete.

WINNING ACTION!

Be Specific. Be Vivid.

What knowledge do I need?

_____

_____

How will I acquire this RIGHT information?

_____

_____

By when will I have this knowledge?

_____

_____

WINNING CONFESSION!

I am enthusiastic about being my best. I will maximize the moment. I will be a great student of the game. I WILL Create the Winning Mindset and become a great athlete. I am a WINNER today!

A WINNING ATHLETE...

When I was drafted in 2011 I knew right away that if I wanted to be the best pitcher that I could possibly be I had to find the right place to train at in the offseason. I asked my friend Dylan Bundy where he was training at and he told me DSD. As soon as he told me I knew I needed to be training there too. Training at DSD with other pro baseball players helps me push myself every day to be better. I can definitely tell by training with this group of guys and the coaches at DSD has benefitted me greatly. I'm stronger, faster, and bigger than I was when I was drafted and that's made becoming a better pitcher easier.

Before I started training with Coach JC and the DSD Coaches I just knew that I wanted to play baseball in the MLB and I'd do anything to get there. After I started training with Coach JC I got more in depth on what exactly I wanted to do while I was playing in the MLB and why I wanted to play so bad. He helped me get out of my comfort zone by having me say "I will do this" or "I will do that" instead of saying "I wish" or "I hope" and to say "I am" instead of "I want to be". By saying these few small things each day, it helped my mind think positive things instead of stuff that could hold me back or make me think that I couldn't do something. It also helped me be more confident in my talent and realize that with my talent I am a lot better than I thought I was. I now use that to make myself better every day.

When I train my mind it's a lot like training my body. I have to train my mind every day just like I do with my body in the weight room. It's not as hard to train your mind as you might think. After learning a few small things from Coach JC it has made training my mind so much easier. I'm thankful for what he and the rest of the DSD Coaches have done for me.

– Adrian Houser, Professional Baseball Athlete

CHAPTER FOUR

WHAT'S MY GAME PLAN

"I visualized where I wanted to be, what kind of player I wanted to become. I knew exactly where I wanted to go, and I focused on getting there."

– Michael Jordan

DO YOU HAVE A GAME PLAN?

All successful people have a plan of action! What's yours? What's your game plan that you will execute to get you to where you need/want to be as an athlete? You have part of your game plan in your hands right now... execute The Create the Winning Mindset game plan that is in your hands right now so that you can get what you desire and deserve.

Now, I want you to put together your own game plan, specific to that thing you desire. For example, if you want to be a successful athlete, what are the components necessary to become that great athlete in your sport? What are you going to do to work on your sport's skill training, strength and conditioning, speed, power, hand quickness, nutrition, supplementation, etc.?

Today, develop your personal game plan. This should be a concrete action plan of the necessary components you will utilize to get what you want. You will need to have a game plan for each of the key areas to get you to your "What".

I want you to think back to the WIN ALL DAY WAY triangle that I shared with you earlier. With "YOU" in the middle as the successful athlete, what components of the triangle must you have a game plan for? ALL three of them!

Today, for you to Create the Winning Mindset, you will create your game plan.

WINNING ACTION!

What areas of training do I need to address?

(List ALL the areas that you must execute for you to have success as an athlete)

_____

_____

What's my game plan in each of these areas?

_____

_____

By when will I have this knowledge?

_____

_____

WINNING CONFESSION!

I am a persistent and diligent athlete. I will work hard each and every day so that I will be a great athlete. I WILL Create the Wining Mindset! I am a WINNER Today!

A WINNING ATHLETE...

"Coach JC understands the power of the mind. I have seen him take average players and turn them into MVP's and All Americans because he made them believe in themselves, get focused, and become the player they should be! He knows how to bring the best out of people and understands how to give them the tools so they can do the same. Whether it's in sports, job, or just life goals Coach JC can give you the tools to have you stop just dreaming about your goals but actually turn those dreams into reality!

"Coach JC as a strength and conditioning coach improved my game on many levels. After being in his program for four years I became a better player. When I came to college I really needed to gain strength and become a better athlete. By training with him I increased my vertical, became quicker and faster, and became much stronger. He not only helped me physically but mentally too. When I doubted myself he would help me push through mental barriers. He helped give me confidence when I needed it and always pushed me to become a better player all around. Because of Jonathan Conneely, "Coach JC" I was able to make it to the next level. Without his training there is no doubt in my mind that I wouldn't be the player I am today."

– *Elisha Turek, Professional Basketball Athlete*

CHAPTER FIVE

TAKE MASSIVE ACTION

"Some people want it to happen, some wish it would happen, others make it happen."

– Michael Jordan

NOW THAT YOU HAVE DEVELOPED YOUR GAME PLAN, IT'S TIME TO TAKE ACTION!

What are your daily action steps to execute your game plan? What is that one, simple, disciplined thing that you will do each and every day to get where you need to be? This is called the Law of Compounding. Time can work for you or against you. This is the step where most athletes fail on the road to success. Most athletes know what they want, but very few athletes' daily actions line up with what they truly desire.

You must break up your game plan into daily action steps. This is how you are going to follow the game plan to get what you truly desire. You have to be very specific here. So, if part of your game plan is to train, your daily action step will be something like, "I will train with my coach at 5:30 A.M. Monday through Friday at the WIN ALL DAY Academy." These action steps answer What, When, Where, and How. Be as specific as possible by listing exact times, locations, and step-by-step-approaches that you will take to get it done. This written itinerary of what, when, where, and how you will do each daily component will transform you into a great athlete.

If you want something you've never had, you've got to do something you've never done.

Willie Mays once said, "In order to excel, you must be completely dedicated to your chosen sport. You must also be prepared to work hard and be willing to accept constructive criticism. Without a total 100-percent dedication, you won't be able to do this."

The Law of Compound is all about DEDICATION and COMMITMENT, my friend.

Mentally tough athletes direct their time and focus on what is important to them in chasing their dreams and goals.

Today to Create the Winning Mindset, you will take massive action in exercising The Law of Compound.

WINNING ACTION!

List EVERY area of your game plan and then list the daily action step that you will do to execute the game plan.

(Be Specific: What, When, Where, How)

*My Daily Action Step For*_____ *is:*

What:

_____

When:

_____

Where:

_____

How:

_____

WINNING CONFESSION!

I am a go-getter. I take massive action and always control my emotions and actions. I WILL Create the Winning Mindset! I am a WINNER Today!

A WINNING ATHLETE...

"Since I came to DSD coach JC has helped me tremendously with the mental side of my game. I had never put much thought into my own mental preparation, which is the biggest part of being a successful athlete. Coach JC has sat down with me on many occasions and really helped me with some simple tools to train my mind for success when I step on the field. These tools helped me tremendously going into my first professional season as a soccer player. I felt more confident than I have ever felt and that led to a very successful rookie season for me. This offseason we have worked even more on mental preparation and mindset and now I am a few weeks out of preseason and I am even more confident than going into last year. Failure is no longer an option and something that never crosses my mind now and I have Coach JC to thank for helping me train my mind to think that way."

– Bryce Taylor, Professional Soccer Athlete

CHAPTER SIX

I DONT ACCEPT FAILURE

"The real glory is being knocked to your knees and then coming back. That's real glory."

– Vince Lombardi

STARTING TODAY TO CREATE THE WINNING MINDSET

and become a GREAT athlete, you won't accept failure anymore! To be a successful athlete you MUST learn how to use failure successfully in your life.

I don't care what happened in the past, and starting today, you don't care either.

Failure is not an option. Today and from here on out, you will establish the no-quit mentality, the no-quit attitude.

The only way that you will ever fail is if you don't finish. There is no other way that you can fail if you have the RIGHT game plan, your daily action steps are executed, and you stick with it!

Now get focused on the prize and Never Quit! Start today and begin to allow your vision to expand!

Once you Create the Winning Mindset you will also find a way to WIN. Winners use losses to drive themselves to become better. Quitters take losses and use them as excuses to quit.

Winston Churchill once said,

"Act as though it were impossible to fail."

Today to Create the Winning Mindset, you will no longer accept failure as an option and you will do this by making a commitment to yourself. Here is the commitment that you will use to hold yourself accountable to sticking with it.

WINNING ACTION!

My Goal(s) is(are)...

1: _____

2: _____

3: _____

"I hereby state that I will abide by my goals listed above. This commitment is between me and me. I know that I can do it! I know that I will achieve them! Failure is not an option! I will not quit until I get there. There is no stopping me! I have the discipline, the determination, and the will to achieve all of my goals! From this day forward I consider it done! I will complete my goals by _____ (date)."

Signature: _____

Date: _____

*Post this in a visible place where you will see it and say it every day.

WINNING CONFESSION!

I am committed to reaching my goals. I can do it and I WILL do it! I am not a quitter and nothing can stop me. I WILL Create the Winning Mindset! I am a WINNER Today!

A WINNING ATHLETE...

"Coach JC Is a one of a kind coach. You will never find someone who pushes you to your complete max, mentally and physically. The reason I started training with Coach JC is because, I knew if I surrounded myself with people who work as hard as they can to make yourself and the people around you better, that I could maximize my potential and get to where I want and need to be!

Prior to training with Coach I never really knew what a workout was. With Coach JC I realized I was in the right place the minute Coach JC started talking! I have never had a coach motivate me at the level he has and will continue to do! It's almost like he's anxious to see us reach our goals, that is what I love to see in my trainer!

Since I've been training with Coach JC at Dynamic Sports Development I have noticed the attention to detail and technique. I have also noticed alot of strength and endurance in my body. When doing a pull-up or a squat for instance Coach JC is right there motivating you to "get the weight up" and every rep completed you'll know it by a "YUP"! I've noticed a totally different mindset when I walk in to DSD!"

– Parker Bridwell, Professional Baseball Athlete

CHAPTER SEVEN

NO MORE EXCUSES

"What's more important: your excuse or what you want?"

– Coach JC

NO GREAT ATHLETE HAS EVER BECOME GREAT BY MAKING EXCUSES.

You will make the choice today to no longer make excuses in your life. You know what they say about excuses!

It's time to take responsibility for YOU! It's your body, your career, your life! This is such a powerful thing because without it you will look at your life as a failure, keep making excuses, and never accomplish your dreams and goals. Once you take responsibility, you will begin to experience peace and joy in your life and take full control over every situation. It's time to be honest with yourself. Starting today, eliminate words like "I can't," or "but" in your vocabulary!

The words you use influence your mind and condition your actions. The words you choose to use will directly determine the direction you go mentally and physically.

Starting today, you must become aware of the words you use and choose to say to yourself. Whenever you hear that voice in your head that says, "I can't," ask yourself two simple questions: Where's the facts and evidence that proves I can't?" "Has anyone else ever been able to make this happen?"

Stop talking yourself out of getting what you truly desire. What's more important: your excuse or your desire?

You can only have excuses or RESULTS, you cannot have both. What do you choose?

Mentally strong athletes become self-motivated and don't accept excuses. Start today to enter every game and training session to WIN. Start today to believe that you are the BEST player in the game. No longer allow yourself to think self- defeating, excuse-making thoughts. I once heard it said, "Don't believe everything you hear, even if you're the one doing all the talking."

WINNING ACTION!

What can I do better?

_____

_____

How can I do more?

_____

_____

What excuses have I been making that I will stop today?

_____

_____

WINNING CONFESSION!

I am a mentally strong athlete. I choose to get RESULTS, and I don't accept or make excuses. I choose to speak positive, uplifting words about my life and my athletic career. I WILL Create the Winning Mindset! I am a WINNER Today!

A WINNING ATHLETE...

"I train with Coach JC because it gives me the chance to be at the top of my game. Not only with the physical part but also mental. The mindset training has helped me realize my want and what I have to do to obtain it. Also the positive influence I need to push myself when times get hard.

The physical aspect of it is that my body has transformed and helped sharpened my skills. I'm stronger leaner and faster thanks to the training with Coach JC."

– David Chester, Professional Baseball Athlete

CHAPTER EIGHT

LET NEGATIVITY GO

"Don't let what you cannot do interfere with what you can do."

– John Wooden

WHAT NEGATIVE INFLUENCES IN YOUR LIFE ARE HOLDING YOU BACK FROM BEING A GREAT SUCCESS AND ACCOMPLISHING YOUR GOALS?

Starting today, it's time to eliminate negativity from your life! You know what I'm talking about! It could be someone or something that you have allowed to beat you up so badly that it has kept you from what you want.

You need to identify those negative things and start today to eliminate them from your life. Maybe you need to break some negative patterns or habits that you have created. These habits could include things you do, read, or watch – things that may be robbing you of your valuable time. Maybe it's someone in your life that has told you, "You can't do it," or maybe it's the environment that you are in on a daily basis that is holding you back.

These negative forces in your life, both internal and external, will continue to drain you and hold you back from what you truly deserve. It all comes down to one word, my friend, CHOICE! Choose today to change the things you are doing, dissociate with negative people, change your environment, and do whatever you need to do to GET WHAT YOU DESERVE!

Great athletes are able to do what they must do to control their emotions and actions. You can't allow outside sources affect you.

Did you know that by the time you graduated from first grade you had heard the word "no" over 40,000 times? That's right! That is in comparison to hearing the word "yes" only 5,000 times. You have been conditioned into a "No" environment. So starting today that has got to change. Start to create your "Yes" environment. Don't accept the thought of no or can't, impossible, maybe, and all these other words that question if it is going to become a reality.

Stay focused on what you can control and get rid those things that are controlling your emotions, distracting your actions, and stealing your concentration. This is one of the reasons why in this game plan, you have a Winning Confession every day; so that you can create your "Yes" environment. Create your "Yes" environment today!

Stop talking yourself out of getting what you truly desire. What's more important: your excuse or your desire?

You can only have excuses or RESULTS, you cannot have both. What do you choose?

Mentally strong athletes become self-motivated and don't accept excuses. Start today to enter every game and training session to WIN. Start today to believe that you are the BEST player in the game. No longer allow yourself to think self- defeating, excuse-making thoughts. I once heard it said, "Don't believe everything you hear, even if you're the one doing all the talking."

WINNING ACTION!

What negative things in my life have been holding me back, and what will I replace them with starting today?

Negative habits?

_____

Replace with

_____

Negative Individuals?

_____

Replace with

_____

Negative Environment?

_____

Replace with

_____

WINNING CONFESSION!

YES! I CAN! I WILL! It's Possible! I am in control of my emotions and my actions. I choose to surround myself with "YES" people! I choose to only go to "YES" places and I choose to create a "YES" state of mind. I WILL Create The Winning Mindset! I am a WINNER Today!

A WINNING ATHLETE...

"When I came to spring training this past year, coaches started asking me, "Man look at you, what did you do? You look great!" This gave me tremendous confidence heading into the 2010 season.

After my knee surgery my senior year (high school) things just weren't right. My body didn't work like it used to. I lost a lot of strength due to my knee surgery that I didn't realize I had lost. Strength/mobility in my hips and shoulders were the main keys for me. Coach JC helped me to better achieve that and it was obvious that things were working in a more fluent, efficient manner once I started throwing in spring training. I believe the training program gave me more strength throughout my body making the opportunity for success much greater. I have cut my body fat nearly in half since I started, all while getting stronger year in and year out.

I started training with Coach JC to give myself the opportunity to be in the best physical condition. Before coming to Coach JC, I was already a hard worker and very dedicated, but I wanted someone to push me to the next level. Four years later, more experienced, I can't say that I regret that decision. Thanks Coach JC."

– Bobby Bundy, Professional Baseball Athlete

CHAPTER NINE

CHECK YOURSELF

"Some people say I have attitude – maybe I do... but I think you have to. You have to believe in yourself when no one else does – that makes you a winner right there."

– Venus Williams

YOU'VE HEARD IT SAID, "SUCCESS STARTS WITH ATTITUDE."

I believe they almost have it right. Your attitude is the second part in the success process and crucial to your success. It all starts in your thinking and your mindset of that success. Your THINKING is what ultimate creates your ATTITUDE, your attitude creates your ACTIONS, your actions will determine your RESULTS, and your results will ultimately dictate your success and what you get out of LIFE.

So why is your attitude so important? You've got it! It's because your attitude directly determines your actions! Your attitude affects the way you feel and how you act. Your attitude will make the difference in how you execute the daily action steps to get to your vision. Your attitude will directly affect your performance. Your attitude reflects who you are, and what is on the inside is what comes out. What kind of RESULTS do you want to get? What kind of LIFE do you want to live? Your attitude is a choice and starting today you will choose to bring the attitude that lines up with getting you to what you desire.

Mentally tough athletes learn how to remain focused through good times and bad times. Even when things are not going your way, you have got to manage your emotions and set yourself up to WIN. To be

GREAT your attitude has got to be one of, "I'll do what I have to do to WIN!"

A winner's attitude is positive in expecting the best even when you don't feel like it. There is an "I can do it" with an expectancy that you WILL achieve your dreams, goals and ambitions.

I once had an athlete client walk into my office and say, "Coach, this whole attitude thing that you talked about... I have been working on it and I don't feel like it is working." I remember this moment like it was yesterday; I paused, looked at him, and said, "Your positive attitude won't work if you don't feel like it's going to work, my man. I can assure you that if you choose a negative attitude... that will work for you every time!"

Your attitude is a choice! Your life will go in the direction that you choose it to go in. You will have what you choose to have. Life is going to happen. Life is not fair and life is not unfair; life is life! You won't always feel like having a winner's attitude, but I can assure you that most of what you get out of life is determined by how you CHOOSE to react to each and every circumstance.

I have heard it said many times, "If you think you can, you will and if you think you can't, you won't. It's YOUR choice!

WINNING ACTION!

My attitude starting today is:

_____

_____

_____

WINNING CONFESSION!

I choose today and each and every day to have a WINNER'S attitude. My attitude starting today will line up with what I desire. I will no longer allow my feelings and situations to determine my attitude for me. I WILL Create The Winning Mindset! I am a WINNER Today!

A WINNING ATHLETE...

"Having a successful life, business or athletic career starts with one thing a champion mindset. Having a champion mindset contains a lot of elements, you must one have the confidence in yourself to succeed. The summer of my senior year in high school I came to Coach JC because I wanted to better myself as an athlete so that I could succeed in not only basketball but also football. I wanted to perform at a state champion level. Coach JC did exactly that. While I was training there were things that I didn't know I could achieve but he instilled in me "To get something you've never had, you HAVE to do something you've never done." Also you have to have confidence in yourself to succeed because if you don't believe it you can't achieve it. I told him at the beginning of the summer that I wanted to make the 5a state playoffs in football and WIN the 5a State

Championship in basketball. That summer was the hardest 3 months of my life, I was physically pushed to my limit everyday. But everyday I was reminded of what I was working for and knowing my goals motivated me to work harder. So I went into football season with an unshakeable confidence that I had no doubt that my team could make the playoffs, and when the season ended we finished the year 8-3 and we made the playoffs for the first time in 25 years! I then went into basketball season with the supreme confidence, but some of my teammates still weren't fully on board. Coach JC came and spoke to my team about a champion mindset and we all bought in to bettering ourselves everyday, and it definitely worked and we reached our ultimate goal by hoisting the gold ball as state champion!"

– Grant Murphy, Collegiate Football Athlete

CHAPTER TEN

CHANGE YOUR THINKING

"Change Your Thinking, Change Your RESULTS!"

– Coach JC

YOU CAN HAVE ANYTHING YOU WANT, ANY TIME YOU WANT IT

Once you Create the Winning Mindset. It all starts in the head, my friend. You are truly only six inches away from getting what you want. It's the six inches from your left ear to your right ear: YOUR MINDSET!

Change Your Thinking...**Change Your Life!**

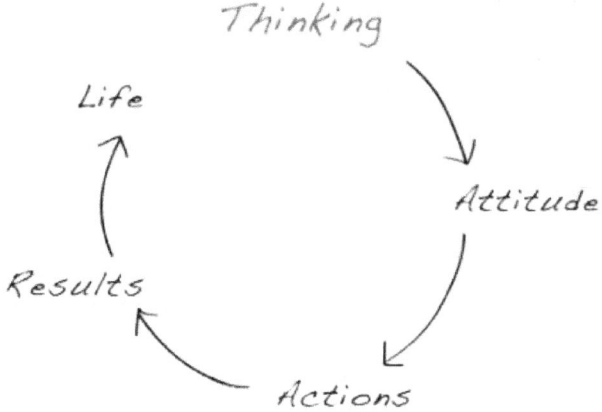

I want you to think about this for a second...

What is that thing you truly desire: that burning desire that you created on day one? Okay, now going off of my "Create the Winning Mindset System" from above, I want you to envision that exact thing where it says LIFE. Check out how simple this really is. Just work your way backwards, and ask yourself: 1) What RESULTS do I need to get to that thing I truly desire? 2) What ACTIONS do I need to take to get me those results? 3) What ATTITUDE do I need to bring every day so my actions line up and BAM! 4) What am I THINKING, what's my MINDSET?! It all starts right there.

Success or failure isn't some big event, my friend. It all comes down to how you think about it. It all starts in your head. So many times we allow others to determine and dictate how we think about ourselves. Over time, these beliefs become a lid on our life to keep us from great success. The power of the mind is incredible! These "limiting beliefs" or "mental barriers" are real and are a lot more powerful than people believe them to be.

Starting today, you must not believe what others – the media, your family members, magazines, other books, co-workers, etc. – are saying. It is time to take the lid off of your life and start to break some records. It is time to think BIG! Change your thinking and you will change your results!

The way you choose to think will affect the way you feel and how you perform. You MUST train your mind to WIN just like you train your body!

WINNING ACTION!

What things in my thinking have been holding me back from ultimate success?

_____

_____

1. *What is it I truly Desire?*

_____

2. *What RESULTS do I need to get?*

_____

3. *What ACTIONS do I need take?*

_____

4. *What ATTITUDE do I need to bring every day so my actions line up?*

_____

5. *What am I THINKING; what's my MINDSET?*

_____

WINNING CONFESSION!

I choose today to think BIGGER! I choose to remove the negative thinking and make a decision on a daily basis to break through my mental barriers so that I can live the life I was born to live! I WILL Create The Winning Mindset! I am a WINNER Today!

A WINNING ATHLETE...

"The Secret to REAL Athlete Success will reinvent the way that athletes approach each day. Half the battle occurs before we even step in the weight-room, pick up a weight, or hit a max lift. The fans know what day the game is, but what they don't see is the work that is put in beforehand. The meetings, film sessions, and countless hours put in on the practice field are the most difficult aspects of being an athlete. We live for game day, and the only way to perform at max potential on game day is to GET YOUR MIND RIGHT FIRST! Coach JC's program has been monumental to my success on the field. The attitude that Coach JC fills the gym with makes me look forward to working out every day. He is the most positive man I know and his constant push in the gym is what helps separate me from my competition. I've grown as an athlete not only physically, but mentally as well because of the way my mind is trained for success now. Because Coach JC has helped me to embrace the daily grind, now I am able to perform at my best on game day."

– Justin Tomlinson, Collegiate Football Athlete

CHAPTER ELEVEN

WHAT AM I REALLY AFRAID OF?

"Most of the things I have accomplished in life have been out of the fear of being mediocre."

– Coach JC

THINK ABOUT IT

How many times have you passed up an opportunity because you were scared of failing? Maybe you were scared of rejection, hearing "no", the pressure, the success, or perhaps, that you just may not be able to do it. Fear can keep you from relationships, opportunities, greater performances, and ultimate happiness and success as an athlete. I've been there! Fear can paralyze you right where you're at and can become your worst enemy if you allow it to.

I want to ask you a question: What are you really afraid of? Are you scared that you won't make it? Are you scared that you may not perform once you do make it? Who cares?! This fear can torture you if you don't take control of it now. This fear will prevent you from achieving ultimate success. Think about how many times in your past you knew that you could have done something but did not act out of fear of failure. Really, think about it, what is the worst that could happen?

The fear of failure actually makes your chance of failing more likely. Fear will force you to play it safe and keep you from making big plays. When you're not afraid to fail, your chances of succeeding increase. You can run from fear or you can attack it head on. Great athletes take the fear of failure and flip the script for it to work for them. Start today to use failure to allow you to learn and grow. Failure can be a great teacher if you allow it to be.

Did you know that you were only born with two fears? That's right! You were only born with the fear of falling and the fear of loud noises. This is great news for you because that means that all other fears have been created, and if you created them, then you can overcome them!

Open book test... Where does this fear of failing come from? You've got it! The same place it all starts: in your THINKING! You cannot allow fear of failure to be part of your thinking, and then allow it to determine your attitude and actions on a daily basis. Instead, you will start to attack these situations in life! Overcoming fear is a two-step process. First, you must detect what this fear is in your life, and second, you must TAKE ACTION on it!

WINNING ACTION!

What has fear kept me from achieving in my life?

What am I afraid of?

What action am I going to take today to overcome this fear in my life?

WINNING CONFESSION!

I choose to not operate in fear but rather in faith. Whatever I put my hand to will succeed. I can do anything I set my mind to and choose to face my fears starting today. I WILL Create the Winning Mindset! I am a WINNER Today!

A WINNING ATHLETE...

"The mentality of an athlete is the most important thing, specially for me. Being mentally tough on the mound is a must for being a good athlete. Coach JC sat me down, was available whenever I needed him, and helped me focus myself on what I wanted to accomplish. Even training physically helped me get the mindset that I have today. Training under Coach JC strengthened me mentally and physically. Out of all the things that I have done, training my mentality was the most important thing. I was taught to never be satisfied, never quit, and of course never quit on your goals in sports, and in life."

– John Lynch, **Collegiate Baseball Athlete**

CHAPTER TWELVE

LIVE, LEARN, AND MOVE ON, BABY!

"You are who you are because of your past choices; who will you choose to be in the future?"

– Coach JC

YOU HAVE A PAST; I HAVE A PAST; WE ALL HAVE A PAST!

Your past can be your worst enemy or your biggest ally! You can allow your past to haunt you and hold you back from great success in athletics and in life, or you can use it to shape you to do great things and get what you deserve.

I have seen many athletes who just could not let go of the past, and they allowed their past to control their future. I don't care what happened yesterday or 10 years ago, it's done! Why allow something that is now out of your control to control you? You may have failed in an outing, you may have not performed at the best of your ability, or you may have just had a bad game... Learn from it and move on, my friend! Don't allow these feelings of depression, guilt, or anxiety control your success. If you live in the past, you will not be able to fully live in the present or in the future. Why be controlled by something you cannot currently control?

We all have situations in our lives that have caused us to become discouraged and develop an attitude of "It's not worth it" or "What's the point in trying any longer?"

Starting today, you will use your past to create future successes. I want you to think of a past situation that may be holding you back right now, and I want for you to ask yourself, what did I learn? You can take any situation, good or bad, and make it a learning experience. These past memories, good or bad, are a part of us. The key is to realize that they are not the reality of who you are right now and then use them to your advantage. So, what did you learn? Maybe there is something you could have done differently to get a different result, maybe you need to put yourself into a different environment, or maybe your reaction to a situation could have been better. What could you have done differently? What did you do wrong? What did you do right? I once heard it said, "A smart man learns from his own mistakes; a wise man learns from the mistake of others!" Learn from it and allow it to propel you to greater success.

You MUST learn to control your emotions

or they will control you!

Now is the time for you to Create the Winning Mindset; time for you to step into your destiny as an athlete; time for you to take control of your career and make those dreams a reality. Now is YOUR Time to Live the Life You Were Born to Live!

WINNING ACTION!

What past situation or situations have been holding me back?

_____

_____

What have I learned from it?

_____

_____

WINNING CONFESSION!

I choose today to allow the past to be the past. I am in complete control and will use past failures to create future successes in my life. I will be the BEST me in the moment and be a difference maker in the lives of others. I WILL Create the Winning Mindset! I am a WINNER Today!

A WINNING ATHLETE...

"Working with Coach JC has helped me to be successful as a Division 1 and Professional Basketball player. His hard work and dedication helped prepare me so that I could play at the highest level.

Coach JC has helped me to become the Athlete that I am today and without him I know that I would not be where I am today. He is the right man for the job. I believe that hard work and dedication is the key to success as an athlete and in life and Coach JC has assisted me in both of these areas.

You choose in life to either be good or great and Coach JC has helped me and pushed me to greatness. Without him I would never be where I am today. I never had alot but I have always been determine to be great and do big things. Coach JC has provided me with an opportunity to be able to do this by pushing me to fight through adversity and obstacles and never allowing me quit.

Coach JC has helped me in preparing for my basketball career and preparing me for the future in life when basketball is over.

Like Coach JC always said, we are only as strong as the weakest link! I never wanted to be the weakest link and Coach JC has set me up to never be the weakest link in basketball or in life."

– *Shawn King, Professional Basketball Athlete*

CHAPTER THIRTEEN

NO QUIT

"Quitting is losing and losing isn't winning!"

– Unknown

IF YOU TRULY WANT TO BE A GREAT ATHLETE, THEN YOU HAVE TO START SEEING YOURSELF AS A WINNER

So many times in life, athletes make the decision mentally to not give 100% effort because of conflict internally. As humans we all have a comfort zone that we try to stay within, and many times we do what we have to do to stay in or get back into that zone. To be a GREAT athlete you MUST get comfortable with being a little uncomfortable. I have seen many athletes allow this comfort zone to limit their momentum and sabotage their success. Not You! Not Any Longer!

Allowing yourself to remain in this comfort zone is tapping out... it's quitting. The one type of person who has always bothered me is the quitter. I cannot stand to see someone just quit and give up! Still to this day, it angers me. Quitting is a mentality and this "quitter mentality" can absolutely prevent you from accomplishing what you really want in life.

Over the last few years in my life and in my coaching business, I have discovered the reason why most people give up. Most people quit because they feel as if they don't have the ability to accomplish what they want or they have to get too far out of their comfort zone to go and get it.

Well, I have GREAT news for you! Did you know that your ability is only 5% responsible for you getting what you truly desire? ONLY 5%! So what's the other 95%, you ask? For you to get the results you desire, create success, get to the next level, become a professional athlete, or just win in life, it all comes down to your... STICKABILITY!

That's my fancy way of saying not quitting! Many people have a problem with following through until the end, and they give up right before they are about to experience a giant breakthrough. Ninety-five percent of getting what you really want in life is just sticking with it, never quitting, grinding it out, and getting a little uncomfortable!

This is so important and can separate you once and for all from your competition. You need to establish a no-quit mentality – a no-quit attitude – so that you can get something you've never had. The key here comes down to the simple, small, daily action steps that you need to be taking each and every day to execute your game plan and to get yourself out of your mental comfort zone. It can't just be when you feel like it or when it's comfortable. You have to make the time, and then stick with it until you get what you want!

Great athletes understand the importance of how they respond. You can't always control the situation and what happens in life, but you CAN ALWAYS control how you choose to react. How you react to the situation will dictate and determine your outcome.

Don't give yourself an out. If you do, you'll use it when times get tough!

Today to Create the Winning Mindset,
it's time you Get Comfortable Being A Little Uncomfortable!

WINNING ACTION!

What have I started that I have given up on?

What am I focused on right now that I will never quit at until I get it?

What areas of my life have I become too comfortable in?

What will I do, starting today, that will be uncomfortable but that I know is necessary for my success?

WINNING CONFESSION!

I am NOT a quitter. I will choose today to get outside of my comfort zone and grow by getting a little uncomfortable. I choose to use situations on a daily basis to make me better, and I will be proactive in how I react to circumstances and situations on a daily basis. I WILL Create the Winning Mindset! I am a WINNER Today!

A WINNING ATHLETE...

"My name is Aaron Mason and I am attending Fort Scott Community College on a baseball scholarship. I started training with Coach JC when he came to my high school baseball practice. I decided at that point this is what I need to further my career in baseball and make it to the next level. Before I started training with Coach JC it was tough for me to last a long time in a ball game. I was never really in shape. I was always struggling keeping up with the other guys on my team. After I started training with Coach JC, I saw results immediately. I started losing weight and body fat. I became more athletic, more in shape, and could keep up with everyone else. Coach JC has taught me many things but the one thing that I will always remember the most is to never give up and always give 110%. I remember we were doing tire jumps and I could never jump on two tires stacked up. Coach JC told me to never quit, to never give up. I finally made the jump after bruising my shins over and over again. Having that mindset of never giving up is not only a sports mindset but a lifestyle. Never give up in life. If you want something bad enough, GO GET IT and like Coach says "Remember why you're here"

– Aaron Mason, Collegiate Baseball Athlete

CHAPTER FOURTEEN

THINK BIGGER

"Beloved, I pray that in all respects you may prosper and be in good health, just as your soul prospers."

– The Bible – 3 John 2

THINK BIG! NOW IT'S TIME FOR YOU TO THINK EVEN BIGGER!

I have the privilege to train some of the top athletes in the world at our sports performance facility, Dynamic Sports Development, in Tulsa, Oklahoma. Many of the athletes that we train have big dreams. It's awesome to see how big they dream: to be great in their individual sports and hopefully play at the next level. When you are doing the necessary things and executing the daily action steps, you should expect big things. What you expect from yourself is what you will get, and what you expect from yourself is what others will expect out of you. Just like the athletes that I train, you now have the right game plan and are executing the daily rituals so you should expect big things and BIG RESULTS! Don't accept being average or mediocre. I don't think you heard me so I'm going to say that one more time... DO NOT accept being average or mediocre! Do ALL you do in excellence! Think Big and Act even Bigger!

You must change your thinking before you can ever become a GREAT athlete. You must BELIEVE you can be GREAT before you ever are. You must believe you can play at the professional level as an athlete before you ever step on that field or court. You must believe you WILL be great each and every time you step into a practice or a train ing session. You have to start to THINK, ACT, and FEEL as if you are already there.

You have to mentally close the deal before you ever have it! You have to see it first in order to ever receive it! Once you see it, you have then got to believe it, and then you will receive it. Don't limit yourself by where you are currently or by what you currently have. You have so much more potential then you even believe you do, my friend! If you don't believe in yourself, why should anyone else?

When you start to THINK BIG and stay focused on the end result, you will find ways to make things happen so that you get what you so badly desire. Most of my clients have adopted the philosophy called, "Fake It 'Til You Make It!" I'm not talking about hoping or wishing; I'm talking about calling it now as what it WILL be!

Fake It 'Til You Make It and start to think bigger today to Create the Winning Mindset and WIN!

WINNING ACTION!

Today you will create your personal I WILL statement. This statement will be a powerful paragraph about those two or three things that you desire. It will include your "What" and your "Why".

You will then place this statement in three different visible areas so that each day you can remind yourself of what you WILL have. Your goal is to say this statement at least three times with authority and actually believe it each time you see it throughout the day. Be specific and vivid, and determine a specific date by which you WILL accomplish this goal.

You can't control your performance until you are in control of your thoughts. What's your mindset?

I WILL

_____

_____

_____

_____

WINNING CONFESSION!

Starting today I WILL expect more out of myself. I'm not average, and I don't think like an average person. I am not mediocre, and I don't do mediocre things. I walk in excellence in ALL I do. In my personal life, in my relationships, and as an athlete, I set myself up for success by THINKING BIG! I WILL Create the Winning Mindset! I am a WINNER!

A WINNING ATHLETE...

CREATE YOUR WINNING STORY.

Today I want for you to create your winning story. You have now heard the success stories from athletes that I have been blessed and privileged to train and help WIN as an athlete and WIN in life.

These athletes are no different than you. They just took this game plan and implemented it. Now it's your turn! Today you will create your future winning success story by writing your current story. On the path to winning all of these athletes have lost. Part of being a GREAT athlete is learning how to use your current situations to create future win's in your life. To WIN you will have to overcome obstacles and adversity on the field and in life. Today I want for you to write down how you currently feel. Your current situation of where you are as an athlete and in life. This will be your before success story. You will look back and be able to see how you created win after win in your life to ultimately WIN! You overcome by creating a testimony, a success story. So right here, right now be honest with yourself and write your current life story.

CHAPTER FIFTEEN

AM I ACCOUNTABLE

"Accountability is making the decision to become REAL with yourself, REAL with what you want and allowing others to make you great by becoming REAL with them!"

– Coach JC

YOU WILL ONLY GO AS FAR AS YOU ARE ACCOUNTABLE!

How are you holding yourself accountable? Who are you allowing to hold you accountable? So many people get uncomfortable when they hear the word accountability. Being accountable is a great thing and a must for you to reach your goals and get what you desire! Look at almost every successful athlete, and you will find that they had true accountability throughout the process in achieving that success.

It will not be easy for you to get what you desire. Nothing worth it in life is easy. Tough times will occur, obstacles will arise, and adversity will come at you; this is when that accountability will be able to pull you through. You have to get accountable!

There will be times when you may not feel like executing your daily actions steps. So what do you do? YOU JUST DO IT! That's right! If you want something you've never had, you can't go by how you feel, my friend! It's a MUST to have that accountability in place to remind you of why you do what you do and to keep you focused on your goal.

This does not mean that I am telling you to trust everyone and anyone. What I am telling you is to find someone who you trust and respect and allow them to make you better. This is someone who wants to see you achieve your goals and live your life to the fullest. No one cares about you getting what you truly desire as much as you, but this person or people may come in a close second to seeing you succeed. This is someone who you can be totally open, honest, and vulnerable with at all times.

Accountability is simple if you're willing to be held accountable. If you think you have arrived or let your pride stand in the way, then this may not be that simple for you.

Here's how it works: you will tell this person your goals and the game plan that you will use to get that thing you desire. Then you will fill them in on what you think is going to be the most difficult part of the process for you. This is where you will ask them to help keep you motivated and focused on the prize and not to let you quit. You will ask them to hold you accountable to your weaknesses and make sure that you are executing your daily action steps. Iron sharpens iron! Who are you going to allow to sharpen you? Who are you sharpening?

Today to Create the Winning Mindset, you will have to make the choice to become accountable to yourself and to others.

WINNING ACTION!

How will I start today to be accountable to myself?

Who will I contact today to allow them to hold me accountable?

WINNING CONFESSION!

Starting today I choose to become accountable to myself and to others. I don't search for the easy way, but rather, I choose to take purposeful action even when I don't feel like it. I choose to just do it! I WILL Create the Winning Mindset! I am a WINNER Today!

A WINNING ATHLETE...

"Coach JC always speaks on the importance of diet and exercise but what you immediately realize when you're around him is that those two elements of success are nothing unless you're in the proper mindset before training even begins. His constant encouragement and support garner a mental outlook in which you believe the only thing you're capable of doing is succeeding. While this begins in the gym, a mindset like this becomes infectious and carries over to the playing field, bringing the same confidence and understanding over to your sport as to your preparation for it. I've seen it in work in my life in a major way over the past three years thanks to Coach JC and his staff and I wouldn't be where I am without it.

Hope that helps, JC. Thank you for everything that you have done for me these last three years and all your support and belief in me. It's helped a tremendous amount and I really appreciate the opportunity to give even a small amount of that back."

– Alex Powell, Collegiate Football Athlete

CHAPTER SIXTEEN

DO YOU FEEL IT?

"Without a sense of urgency, desire loses its value."

– Jim Rohn

DO YOU FEEL IT?

How badly do you want to get to the next level? How badly do you want to make your dream a reality? Do you have a sense of urgency?

Those athletes who make things happen in life are those that posses a sense of urgency. A sense of urgency is established when something is of great importance to you, it is a necessity. You have got to have it. A lot of times this sense of urgency can bring some pressure, but if you want to do anything worthwhile, you'd better learn to appreciate a little pressure. Pressure demands that you get it done. Pressure is knowing that when you wake up in the morning you must find a way to make it happen. Pressure is lying down at night and creatively thinking of ways to make it happen.

Starting today, you need to feel that accomplishing your desire is a matter of life and death.

To be a great athlete you will have to learn how to play under pressure. Why do some athletes break under pressure while others thrive? Pressure is internal; it comes from within and once you understand that the only pressure you're under is that which you've placed on yourself, you will achieve success. Pressure can bring out the best in you, and possessing that sense of urgency can be used as a positive force to drive you to succeed.

In my own life, a lot of the things I've accomplished were due to the fact that I had a sense of urgency – I had to have or needed that thing. I distinctly remember when I started to develop the attitude that I would rather be dead then live a mediocre life. It is now or never!

This attitude motivated me to go get things that I so badly desired and motivated me to avoid that pain of looking back with regret one day. As athletes, your "Why" is the thing that will keep you motivated. You see, everything you do in life is for one of two reasons: to avoid pain or to gain pleasure. Many athletes are motivated by both, and to be a GREAT athlete, you must be motivated to pursue that thing that will bring you pleasure and to avoid that thing that will bring you pain.

It is this kind of motivation through which you will develop a sense of urgency that will propel you in the right direction and keep you moving in the right direction!

What motivates you? How badly do you really want it?

You're on a mission and you will find a way to make it happen.

This is why I provide you with a 27-day game plan. This is not just another book that you read only when it's comfortable. Get it done in 27 days. Period! That is why I provide you with 27 daily action steps, so that you can stop procrastinating and get what you desire as an athlete!

Placing time limits on areas of your life will force you to establish that sense of urgency. You are creating this game plan over the next 27 days to give yourself a sense of responsibility and accountability. It is also to ensure that the necessary steps are completed each day to get you to your ultimate destiny.

Take action today, and stay focused on the task at hand. Realize what is at the end of the tunnel. See the end result! How badly do you really want it? How urgent is it to you?

WINNING ACTION!

Visualize the end result; how urgent is this mission to me?

_____

_____

What is the pain that I am I motivated to avoid?

_____

_____

What is the pleasure that I am motivated to gain?

_____

_____

What will I put timelines on in my life starting today??

_____

_____

WINNING CONFESSION!

I will stay focused and motivated on the end result and approach each day with no regret. I am grateful that the past is the past and I can start new today! I find ways on a daily basis to make it happen. It's now or never and I choose to maximize the moment! I will stay focused and attack each day as I am on a mission to fulfill what I know I was called to do on this earth. I WILL Create the Winning Mindset! I am a WINNER Today!

A WINNING ATHLETE...

"Coach JC's Gameplan delivers the truth about how the mind is an incredibly powerful weapon. It shows you how mastering your mindset can be the tool to obtaining anything that you want in life. The power of my mind has been the engine that has driven me through all life's obstacles, both on and off the court. "The Secret To Real Success" is the coaching that will change your life forever."

– Samuel Dalembert, Professional Basketball Athlete

CHAPTER SEVENTEEN

GET BACK IN THE RACE

"For a race to be finished, you must first start."

– Unknown

I'M A BIG FAN OF FINISHING.

You will never finish if you quit. You will never quit if you don't choose to quit. You can't win a race if you don't finish, right?

Ask any runner and they will tell you that it's not about how you start but how you finish. That is true, but how will you ever finish if you don't start?

Are you in the race? So many times in life we, as athletes, drop out of our race and never get the chance to see the prize at the finish line. Have you been knocked out of the race? Have you dropped out? If things don't start right, you can't just give up, you have to keep running.

Maybe you have tried to become a great 3-point shooter, maybe you have tried to become a great hitter, maybe you have even hired professionals to help train you, but you didn't see results, so you dropped out of the race. Maybe you were cut from the team so you gave up on the sport and the dream.

Did you know that Michael Jordan was cut from his high school basketball team? That's right, the greatest basketball player of all time didn't even make the team, but it didn't stop him. Did you know that a guy named Walt Disney was told at his first trade show that he wasn't creative enough? That's right, look at all that he has created. Disney

World is one of the world's greatest vacation destinations; you may have even been there. So, what's your excuse? You don't have one!

Today, I want you to get back into the race. Maybe this game plan is the starting point for your race. To finish the race, you first have to start the race. I don't care what has happened in the past; your new race begins today. Today is the day you get back into the race – the race of life. Think of every day of your life as just one lap in the competition of your race. Once that lap is over you will never get it back, and once the race is over, it's over. Life is short and once it is over, it is over. There is not another race.

As an athlete your window of opportunity is small and you must maximize each day to the fullest. This always makes me think of my favorite movie, Rocky. In Rocky III, when Rocky is training, Apollo Creed reminds him that there is no tomorrow. Live today like it's your last... give it ALL you've got as you are never promised tomorrow!

That thing you desire is at the finish line, but how badly do you want it? Today, I want you to re-submit your name, put your sneakers on, and get back into the race. Once you get back in, then you will have a chance to win the race. You must refuse to be knocked down; you must refuse to be knocked out. Keep running, my friend, don't look back, stay focused on the end result... that finish line!

This book was created to not only get you back into the race but to take you all the way to the finish line!

WINNING ACTION!

In what area of my life have I dropped out of the race? (Mental, Physical, Spiritual, etc.)

_____

_____

What do I need to do today to get back into the race?

_____

_____

What do I see at the finish line?

_____

_____

WINNING CONFESSION!

I choose to get back into the race. I am not a quitter and I choose to not quit. I will live today as if it were my last and enjoy every moment. I choose to create fun in my life and run my race. I WILL Create the Winning Mindset! I am a WINNER Today!

A WINNING ATHLETE...

"The training program with Coach JC has advanced my game and has put me in a position to be a very rich man!!"

– Caleb Green, Professional Basketball Athlete

CHAPTER EIGHTEEN

ALL DAY!

*"If you don't believe in yourself,
why should anyone else believe in you?"*

EXPECT RESULTS! ALL DAY!

Preparation time is never wasted time, my friend, and if you are doing the things necessary to get what you desire, then you should expect results. I always tell my athletes: the ones who are disciplined, dedicated, determined and who put the time into training and preparing SHOULD EXPECT good things. You should expect results. ALL DAY! Once you start to implement the program and implement it to the fullest, then you should expect to see the results you desire.

The mind is a powerful weapon. If you don't believe in yourself, then why should anyone else believe in you? I am not talking about being cocky and arrogant. I am talking about CONFIDENCE: a confidence that you are taking care of business, that you are back in the race, and that you are not going to quit until you reach your final goal. The only one who can take you out of the game is yourself. While you are on the field you can't be defeated, while you are on the court you can't lose, while you are in the race you are the best on the track. Remember the only one who can take you out of the race is you!

Start expecting results, start expecting good things, and start expecting your life to take a turn in the right direction! You can now have the peace of mind of knowing that you have the Secret to REAL Athlete Success. The time of doubting yourself is over! Expect great things in your life, and expect that you will see the results you desire. Have confidence that you can do it, and you will have great success as an athlete. Expect to be the BEST! Expect to get to the Next Level! Expect To Get What You Came For! Expect results knowing that you are doing what is right. Expect results now that you are taking the risks needed to take control of your athletic career and future.

As an athlete you have to expect just a little more, you have to do just a little more, and you have to have faith that it's all going to work out and that you have what it takes. I remember a specific scene from the movie, Facing the Giants, when the football coach challenges Brock to bear-crawl to the 50-yard line. Then he has his teammate get on his back and even blindfolds him as he bear crawls. When asked why, his reply, "I don't want you giving up when you can go further!"

If you haven't seen this movie you may want to, but Brock winds up making it all the way to the end zone. He bear-crawled the entire football field blindfolded with his teammate on his back. Just like Brock you have to expect more and start giving just a little more. You have been gifted with a talent; don't waste it. You can't give up on yourself and not fulfill your destiny. Start today to remove the doubt and obstacles that are holding you back in your own mind.

You now have the game plan that you need to do it. You have committed to finishing the race, and you are focused on the end result. Now is the time to expect results; never doubt that you can do it! Start to THINK, ACT, and FEEL as if you are already there. See It, Believe It, and Expect It to come to pass.

Starting today, I want you to adopt the "ALL DAY" mentality. The "ALL DAY" mentality is the mentality that you will do and are doing what it takes each and every day to Get What You Came For. If you have ever been around me while coaching, chances are you have heard me yell out at some time, "ALL DAY!" This is my way of building up an athlete's confidence in reminding him that he has what it takes and nothing can stop him unless he allows it to. ALL DAY is the mentality that I have more and can do more and I WILL NEVER QUIT!

I believe in you! Believe in yourself! ALL DAY!

WINNING ACTION!

In what area of my life have I dropped out of the race? (Mental, Physical, Spiritual, etc.)

What do I need to do today to get back into the race?

What do I see at the finish line?

WINNING CONFESSION!

I choose to get back into the race. I am not a quitter and I choose to not quit. I will live today as if it were my last and enjoy every moment. I choose to create fun in my life and run my race. I WILL Create the Winning Mindset! I am a WINNER Today!

A WINNING ATHLETE...

"I was looking for someone who understood the complexity of muscle building without adding bulk that interferes with a boxer's ability to punch and move. I'm a tall guy at 6'6" and with the daily 5-7 hour workouts it gets tough to keep the muscle on and keep the injuries away – JC introduced nutrition and stretching into my workout routine.

Prior to training with Coach JC I did a lot of running and weight training – movements that aren't natural during an athlete's performance. JC was able to incorporate muscle building into movement and the result was a significant performance improvement reflected in my coordination, speed, punching ability and stamina. Since training with Coach JC I Improved coordination, speed, punching ability and stamina. Stronger core/trunk/legs and not just for show – the muscles are built with movement and purpose.

When you train 7 hours a day often the challenge becomes getting excited about what you do day in and day out – just like any professional in every career. JC always has a positive attitude and it's very motivating and sometimes being around a motivational person to remind you of your goals is key to unleashing a productive workout.

In preparing for a fight, confidence is KING. You have to know that everything you've done leading up to a fight has prepared you for stepping into the ring with your opponent. Beyond that though is a fighters journey to the top which is never a direct route – there are so many twists turns ups and downs and you have to have some serious gumption to ride the wave. You have to set your goals from the start and never lose sight of them – especially when things get tough.

I was never a natural athlete – being tall and lanky my coordination as a kid was terrible and I had to work very hard to be good at sports. This is pretty much what shaped me as an athlete – nothing was ever easy but I knew if I worked really hard I could turn my weaknesses into strengths. It's that belief in myself that the sky is the limit if I work hard that still propels me."

– Wes Nofire, Professional Boxer

CHAPTER NINETEEN

SEPARATE YOURSELF!

---

*"Be not deceived; God is not mocked:
for whatsoever a man soweth, that shall he also reap."*

– Galatians 6:7

WHAT I SOW IS WHAT I SHALL REAP!

This is not just some spiritual saying from the Bible but a universal law in life. I have found it to be very true in many different aspects of life. "What you sow, you will reap." If you sow badly, you will reap badly; if you sow good stuff, you will reap the reward. If all you eat is junk food, you will reap the negative effects of that junk food. If you sow the time to train and work on your skill, you will become a better athlete. As you start to follow the game plan, you will reap the benefits of being one step closer each day to your goal.

Everyone wants to be successful, but those who achieve that success are sowing the right seed every single day. Those successful athletes that I have worked with are disciplined and determined to have that success. They do what they have to do, when they have to, even when they don't feel like doing it. Having a big dream is not enough. You must be a driven, self-disciplined athlete who accepts no excuses and has complete resolve to execute the daily rituals until you get there. This is how you SEPARATE YOURSELF!

How much time are you sowing into getting what you want? How much effort are you sowing into your daily action steps to get what you desire? What do your daily rituals look like?

It's not just about doing it but doing it the right way. You've probably heard it said: practice makes perfect. Not necessarily! Practice makes permanent. Practicing the RIGHT way makes perfect. Perfect practice makes perfect! Are you sowing the right seed? Are you practicing the RIGHT way? Stop wasting your time staying busy and start investing your time wisely by being productive! Start today to make sure that you are sowing the RIGHT seed on a daily basis to get you to reap the ultimate reward as an athlete. This is how you SEPARATE YOURSELF!

To be a successful athlete you have got to eliminate distractions on a daily basis. I have met so many athletes that lead schizophrenic lives. They say they want one thing but are just not willing to do what it takes and discipline themselves. Don't be deceived in thinking these distractions will not take you off of your road to success. Align your actions with your words, and start today to sow the right seed so that you can reap the reward. This is how you SEPARATE YOURSELF!

If You Want Something You've Never Had,

You've Got To Do Something You've Never Done!

Know your PURPOSE! Live it with PASSION! Become PERSISTENT! and PLAY each and every day with MASSIVE ACTION! This is how you SEPARATE YOURSELF!

WINNING ACTION!

Am I sowing good seed on a daily basis to get what I desire?

What can I do better or more of to reap what I desire?

What am I going to do that I've never done so that I can get what I've never had?

WINNING CONFESSION!

Starting today I choose to SEPARATE myself. I will sow only the right seed so that I can reap the reward. I know my purpose and choose today to live with passion and purpose and persistence so that I can SEPARATE myself. I choose to take massive action and believe the best is yet to come in my life and as an athlete. I WILL Create the Winning Mindset! I am a WINNER!

A WINNING ATHLETE...

"Prior to training with coach JC and his team at DSD I was just an average athlete with huge goals and ambitions but no way to accomplish them. I decided to train at DSD after my first trial week, during that week I noticed the mental strength of the athletes who trained there and that as an athlete that was something I desperately needed but did not have. After the last three years at DSD not only have I improved physically in enormous ways but more importantly I have been able to train my mind on what it is to win every day in all of the things I do. The most common problem with athletes is their mind, they do not know how to win and they do not know what it is to have the right mind set about training and playing and the great advantages that come with having the right thoughts and ideas. Training with coach JC and his team has taught me to be a better man in my every day life, I have learned to teach others how to win and how to get their mind right so that they can win as well. My experiences at DSD have changed my life and there is no way I could have been where I am today without coach JC and his team."

– Andrew Wyrrick, Collegiate Hockey Athlete

CHAPTER TWENTY

BE A CONTROL FREAK

"First we make our habits; then our habits make us."

– Charles C. Noble

YOUR FUTURE IS IN YOUR HANDS

You control your future, and you determine what happens now, tomorrow, and forever. You are where you are today because of the decisions you made yesterday. You will be who you are in the future based on the decisions you make today. I talk to so many athletes who have allowed other people and other people's situations to determine where they are currently. It's time you take responsibility for your actions. No one forces you to do what you do, and no one forces you not to do it. You are in complete control of your life, and now by lining up your daily rituals you can change your life forever.

Many athletes allow their bodies to get so out of shape and don't want to take control for the outcome. No one made you eat fast food every day! You are at this point in your life today because of the choices that you made yesterday. You control your future, and you control your life. Be a control freak. It's your life! It's your career! Take control of it!

This is why your desire, your "WHAT", must be strong; it must be strong enough to overcome mental laziness. Some athletes want the easy way out because they have allowed their mental laziness to create an attitude of laziness, which has produced daily laziness in their actions. This is easy to do if you're not careful. NOT YOU! Do not allow mental laziness to determine your future. I won't let you do it. Not anymore!

You have to make a choice to no longer blame others for where you are at in life and to no longer complain about what you don't have. You must make the choice to overcome mental laziness. You control it, my friend! Stop settling because it's comfortable or easy at the moment.

Are you sacrificing what you want most in life for what you want at the moment?

You know what you want! Is what you want at the moment more important than getting what you want most in life? Do you want that starting position more than that late night party? Do you want to get drafted more than you want to look cool and fit in? Do you want that professional contract or that late night at the club? Do you want the result or the excuse? It's your choice, you control the outcome.

Your future is created NOW in the present! You must take purposeful action each day so that you can maximize the moment. This is how you WIN! Remember, winning is the daily ritual or habit that you do to get you closer to your "WHAT". Start today to be in control of your life and no longer allow adversity, obstacles, distractions, haters, or anything else to steal your dream.

WINNING ACTION!

What areas of my life have I been allowing others to control?

_____

_____

What do I want most in life?

_____

_____

What will I do in my life to not allow mental laziness to control my future?

_____

_____

WINNING CONFESSION!

I choose to no longer allow excuses to stop me. I am a go-getter! I am an overcomer! I am a mentally strong, determined, focused athlete and person. I never settle and don't want the easy way but rather the right way! I choose to take purposeful action each and every day. I WILL Create the Winning Mindset! I am a WINNER!

A WINNING ATHLETE...

"Coach Jonathan Conneely (Coach JC) is one of the greatest coaches I've had the privilege to bless my game. He taught the true meaning of hard work, dedication To the body, and how to use every bit of potential one has stored in him/herself. I met Coach JC as my strenght and conditioning coach at Oral Roberts University. In the weight room, we had a couple quotes that stuck.. When coach said "get big son" i would reply with "YOU KNOW!" After every workout. He pushed uspassed the limit we thought we could go. He showed me there isnt a limit, but a mental illusion of self limitation. After meeting coach John and continuing my basketball career after ORU, all the hard work and mental trails endured with Coach JC has pushed me passed the "limit". Here i am now playing professional basketball and traveling the word (8countries visited). All because of a mind set that keeps me fighting for more. I give true thanks to my coach and friend Jonatan Connelly."

– *Sylvester Spicer, Professional Basketball Player*

CHAPTER TWENTY ONE

TAKE THE LID OFF

"You can have anything you want, any time you want it, once you change your thinking!"

– Coach JC

IT WAS MAY 6, 1954

and no runner competing in track and field had ever run a mile in less than four minutes. All the so-called experts and commentators declared that it would never be done. Studies were performed to show that it was not humanly possible and that no one could possibly run that fast for that long in order to make it happen. For years those tests and studies stood true, and no one broke the four-minute-mile barrier. However, on that day in 1954, a man named Roger Bannister made sports history and ran a mile in 3 minutes and 59 seconds! Up until that point, the runners had allowed the opinions of others to dictate their outcome. Roger Bannister trained hard and did not believe what all the experts were saying. He did not believe that it was impossible. He refused to let others determine his outcome, and he believed that he would break that four-minute-mile limit. He did not allow others to put a limit on his life. He was going to determine his own future and his own destiny.

This story is so fascinating, not only because Roger Bannister made history, but also because of what I am about to tell you: just 46 days later, another runner broke his record. Now, after more than 50 years, hundreds of runners have run a mile in less than four minutes! I want you to think about that. For hundreds of years no one could run the mile in less than four minutes. It was pretty much accepted that no man could break the four-minute-mile barrier. It was believed that the four-minute mile was physically impossible. It was commonly accepted as a fact! However, the reality was that the four-minute mile was a psychological barrier!

So what happened? I will tell you. For all those years, athletes allowed others to set that barrier in their minds. For all those years runners believed what others said. Everyone was convinced that it was impossible. The lid was put on their abilities. The power of the mind is incredible! These "limiting beliefs" or "mental barriers" are real and are a lot more powerful than people believe them to be.

I am here to tell you that you can't believe everything that others are saying: the media, your family members, magazines, other books, coaches, teammates, etc. It is time to start to break some records. It is time to THINK BIG! Change your thinking and you will change your results. It's time to throw the lids off of your life!

WINNING ACTION!

What is the four-minute-mile barrier in my life or as an athlete?

What things in my thinking have been holding me back from ultimate success as an athlete?

WINNING CONFESSION!

I choose today to run the race to win. I choose today to let go of the psychological barriers in my life. I choose today to remove the lids that have been placed on my life. I choose today to break through and no longer accept average, mediocre, or subpar performance. I choose to think BIG and act BIGGER today. I WILL Create the Winning Mindset! I am a WINNER!

A WINNING ATHLETE...

"I HAD IT ALL! (or at least I thought I did) I was a very successful collegiate baseball pitcher. I was a 2-time All-American. I held multiple NCAA records. I had more trophies than losses. I was close to signing professionally twice, and all of that came to a screeching halt. I had no idea what to do. Imagine having one dream your entire life, then being told that dream is not possible anymore. Luckily, I set myself up academically to get accepted into the Baylor University Graduate School. My best friend then introduced me to the city of Tulsa & I fell in love immediately. I found Coach JC, and when I met him, God gave me this overwhelming feeling that I needed to be around him, some how, some way. Talk about divine appointment!

I came to Coach JC depressed, lost, & extremely overweight. The only life I knew was Baseball; it was my identity. I was a winner in Baseball, & nothing else. Coach JC pushed my limits day after day and helped me realize the potential that I have. He showed me how to transfer the valuable skills I learned through baseball into every aspect of my life. Now, I have lost over 60 pounds, and I am doing things I've never done before. To top it all off, I am walking out my purpose every single day! He has changed my life forever!

There is no greater power than the words you speak into your life! The words you speak will train your thoughts, and your thoughts will spark action - good or bad. It's time to take control of your life, and the first step in doing so is reading this book, and TRUSTING the system Coach JC has laid out for you! If it worked for me, it WILL work for you."

– Riley Tincher, Collegiate Baseball Player,
Strength & Conditioning Coach

CHAPTER TWENTY TWO

HOW'S MY AGILITY?

"Don't let obstacles stop you. If you run into a wall, don't turn around and give up, figure out how to climb it, go through it, or work your way around it.

Do whatever it takes to make it happen!"

– Coach JC

ARE YOU READY? YOU'D BETTER BE!

Obstacles are going to occur, times are going to get tough, the road will be rocky, adversity will arise, and uncomfortable times will happen. This is a guarantee, my friend. The question is not, will it ever happen? Instead, the question is: "What am I going to do when these inevitable circumstances occur?" Starting today, YOU NEED TO BECOME AGILE. Being agile is a huge component of being a great athlete. We train our athletes to become more agile so that they can perform at the highest level. You have probably even worked on some specific drills to increase your agility as an athlete. You prepare now so that you have the skill necessary when the competition comes.

Circumstances happen, both good and bad in life. Some you can control, and others you just can't control. How will you react? The name of the game is to prepare how you will react to these circumstances when they come. How you react will determine the outcome. The best thing you can do during these trials and tribulations is to stay positive and optimistic. This won't be easy, but you have to make the choice to not be moved by how you feel. I have heard it said that "successful people look at setbacks in life as opportunities for a comeback."

Stay resilient and refuse to lose!

Agility is defined as the ability to get from point A to point B in the shortest amount of time, while losing the least amount of motion. For you to be successful and to accomplish what you desire, you will need to become agile both physically and mentally. When your mind becomes agile, you will be able to conquer anything. Watch how quickly the results start to occur! Watch the mindset you create, the success you start to experience, and the life you start to live. What are you going to do when obstacles come at you? You have to do whatever it takes to not let them stop you.

Nothing can stop you! I don't care if you have to go through, around, over, or under. Whatever you have to do, you must do it. This is something that is developed; increasing your mental agility can be trained just like physical agility as an athlete. You must make a conscious effort on a daily basis to fight through obstacles and not react based on how you feel but rather in the way that will get you the outcome you desire. Every day a situation will arise that will make you uncomfortable, so practice becoming more agile. Use daily circumstances to make yourself better so that when the large obstacles are thrown at you, you will know how to react.

Starting today I want you to learn how to become comfortable becoming uncomfortable.

WINNING ACTION!

How will I choose to react to situations so that I will get the outcome I desire?

How will I become comfortable today becoming uncomfortable?

What area of my life do I need to become more agile and persevere through?

WINNING CONFESSION!

Nothing can stop me! I choose today to become agile and not allow circumstances to dictate and determine how I react. I choose to react mentally and physically with the end result in mind. I will create a way to persevere through and stay persistent in reaching my goals. I WILL Create the Winning Mindset! I am a WINNER!

KINNY SPOTWOOD

"Coach JC has helped me not only in my physical training but helping me train mentally so i am at my peak before a fight, having an mental winning mindset is just an important physical preparation. Coach JC will push you mentally to help build you up as a complete athlete so you are able to push further then ever ..... I am grateful to have the opportunity to work with him."

– Kinny Spotwood, Collegiate Football Athlete, MMA Fighter

CHAPTER TWENTY THREE

DETERMINE YOUR PRIORITIES

"You can always tell what people really want in life by looking at their priorities."

– Coach JC

WHAT ARE YOUR PRIORITIES?

Do you know why a lot of athletes are underachieving and never experience optimal results? Do you know why so many athletes wish and hope to make money as a professional athlete but never make it? Why so many kids dream of being a professional athlete but never achieve it? It's simple... It's because doing the daily action steps to get them to their goal was never made a priority. What is it that you really value in life? You can always tell an athlete's desires and values by looking at his priorities. What are your priorities?

Now is the time to address the priorities in your life! I'm not talking about what you may say your priorities are but rather what your actions really reflect. Your priorities are not expressed by what you say; they are determined by your daily actions. You may know in your heart that you want to be great, make the varsity squad, be an Olympian, be an All-star, but that doesn't matter... it's the follow through, the action, that is slowing down your progress. Starting today, you will need to make sure that what you ultimately want becomes a priority in your daily actions steps.

WINNING ACTION!

Coach JC's Five Steps to Prioritize Your Priorities:

1. Know what you want – don't waiver from it. What Do I want?

_____

_____

2. Write it out – Make it clear and be specific and realistic. What are my Top 5 Priorities in getting what I want?

_____

_____

3. Live it out – Walk it out on a daily basis. Be who you say you are! Who am I?

_____

_____

4. Associate Yourself – Surround yourself with people who have similar priorities. Who will I surround myself with?

_____

_____

5. Give it a check-up – Re-evaluate your priority list on a monthly basis. When will my scheduled check-up be each month?

_____

_____

WINNING CONFESSION!

I choose today to align my priorities in my life with what it is I ultimately want. I will dream big and act even bigger. I am valuable in life and I am worth it. I choose today to value time. Each and every day, I will be a go-getter so that I can reach my goals and leave a legacy. I WILL Create the Winning Mindset! I am a WINNER!

A WINNING ATHLETE...

"Softball is my passion! And JC has helped make me a better athlete. I started out as a 120 pound, skinny armed player hitting mostly singles. I now weigh 135 pounds, have gained muscle and am hitting lots of doubles and home runs. JC hasn't only helped my body but also my mind. He has helped me realize that the game is just as mental as it is physical. JC has taught me how to keep a positive mind set and stay relaxed, which has helped during the occasional hitting slump. It is my "circle of excellence"! I have to focus on what I want to happen. JC always make me feel like a SUPER STAR! With his help, I know I will achieve my dream of playing college softball."

– Erin Skinner, Competitive/ high school softball player

CHAPTER TWENTY FOUR

SET YOUR GOALS

"Setting goals is the first step in turning the invisible into the visible."

– Anthony Robbins

IF YOU DON'T KNOW WHAT YOU WANT, YOU WILL NEVER GET IT

If you don't know where you are going, you will never get there. Setting goals will help lead you to where you want to go in life. That's what this whole book is about: discovering what you want and taking the necessary daily action to go and get it!

Knowing where you want to go will enable you to concentrate your daily activities, actions, and efforts on the things that are necessary to get there. Setting goals help solidify what the expectation truly is and help you to start to see yourself in a better way with increased confidence.

I am never amazed when I sit down with a client and ask him, "What are your goals?" He may say to play in the NBA, to play in the NFL, to pack on 25 pounds of muscle, to earn that Division I scholarship, to be an All-American. Most athletes don't even need to think about it. A lot of athletes have determined their ultimate long-term goal, and that is great. I then follow up by asking him, "What are you doing right now to get there?" Very few people set short-term goals. Where do you need to be in the next 30 days, what about the next 90 days?

These short-term goals are the small rewards leading to the big prize at the end. Once you have determined these short-term goals, the question is: what do you need to do on a daily basis? What about on a weekly basis? Or even a monthly and annual basis to get to this ultimate goal?

Goal setting is crucial, but without the game plan to get you there, you will never complete those goals. Goals will keep you on target and help you to stay focused on what it is you want. Setting goals will push you to take action and improve your performance by bringing your future to your present.

In this book, starting today, you are going to set goals and have fun doing it. Setting goals is what will turn your dreams into actions so that you can make them a reality.

Set goals that you know you can control the outcome of by taking the right action. Let these goals be a challenge to you but also make them realistic. Your goals should be big enough that you have to work for them. They should be things that get you pumped and excited to chase and inspire you to never quit.

WINNING ACTION!

Goals Are Dreams With Timelines. Be specific. Be Realistic. Have a timeline.

My Ultimate Goal is

_____

and I will accomplish this by _____ (date)

My 1-year Goal is

_____

and I will accomplish this by _____ (date)

My 90-day Goal is

_____

My 30-day Goal is

_____

WINNING CONFESSION!

I know what I want, and I won't quit until I get it. I stay focused on my goals, and I do what it takes each day to get me closer to my goals. I am a determined, focused, disciplined athlete. I'm excited about my present and my future. I create fun in ALL I do as an athlete. I WILL Create the Winning Mindset! I am a WINNER!

A WINNING ATHLETE...

"Coach JC, you and the DSD speed and strength staff have helped me climb to new levels- and those levels represent an outlook on myself as an athlete. You've shown me how to get to that next level of speed, power, and mental focus that it takes to compete in division one athletics. A summer at DSD with Coach JC helped me reach a new level of play that I hadn't seen before and it felt incredible. The mental focus- the mindset it takes to compete in collegiate football has to be fine tuned and precise so that you always remember why you play the game. And having that dialed in mindset focused on whatever it goal it may be in huge when competing like it is your full time job. Being a student athlete it is important to have a mindset that is driven towards nothing but success and knowing how to over come adversity is just as important. Coach JC places emphasis on why you work and why you put your body through the sweat and the pain when he coaches- and he constantly reminded me to take it personally when it came to working with everything I've got training to be faster and more powerful."

– Corbin Stall, College Football Athlete

CHAPTER TWENTY FIVE

DECIDE TO SPEAK IT

"All our dreams can come true if we have the courage to pursue them"

– Walt Disney

THIS IS ALWAYS A FUN AND DIFFICULT STEP FOR ATHLETES TO DO.

I want you to begin to speak those things that you desire and want to accomplish in life. Let me start by saying that I don't believe you can just repeatedly say that you want something and it will happen. I am talking about speaking with a confidence and a positive attitude, while at the same time believing without a doubt that those things that you are taking action on will come to pass.

Faith comes by hearing; this is why in each chapter of this book, I provide you with a Winning Confession to repeat daily. It helps build up that faith.

If you repeatedly say, "I am going to play varsity as a midfielder!" Then you will subconsciously find ways to make yourself get to that place. You will start to believe that it is already a reality; therefore, you'll do what's necessary to make it happen. There is tremendous power in your words, my friend. This can also work against you if you allow it. If you keep saying, "I'll never make the team," you won't make any effort, and you will eventually quit because your subconscious mind will have accepted that you will never get there.

The other reason that this is so powerful is that you will have people who will speak against you accomplishing your goal, people who do not want you to succeed, and people who will doubt that you can do it. Haters will be haters. The way to counteract this negativity is for you to defeat them by speaking what you desire into existence. When you speak against this negativity, you are releasing your confidence, and you are exposing yourself to positive energy.

You will never really experience true success as an athlete if you are negative and are always speaking depressing and doubtful things. When you constantly speak negatively, it will make you unpleasant to be around and very unhappy. Who wants to be around those kinds of people? I am a big action guy, and you should feel confident to do this because you are putting action behind the words! Here is the cool thing: speaking your goal into existence can considerably improve your results and how you feel about yourself, your goals, and others.

It goes back to the premise that what you sow is what you will reap. Now, why is this so powerful for you? It is because you are not only speaking it, but you are putting action behind it while you speak it. Here's what I mean: I want you to not just speak it, but SPEAK IT WITH AUTHORITY. Say it like you mean it. Use the tones and pitches in your voice; use the non- verbal communication of your body language to express what you really want. Speak it with visualization and imagination and start to see that very thing that you are speaking! That is what the game plan is all about, and that is a powerful combination!

It always makes me laugh when someone says that there is no power in words. Think about it for a second... Think about something someone said to you as a kid that was hurtful. Chances are you can probably recall something that was said. You have never forgotten it! In fact, it may even still bother you. Maybe someone told you that you couldn't do something. Then you started to think that maybe you couldn't, and it stopped you from accomplishing something in your life. On the flip side, has anyone ever said something so positive to you that it encouraged you to take a step in your life that you were afraid to take? I know that this has happened to me.

There's Power in Your Words! YOUR belief will drive your behavior and your behavior will dictate your performance. Change your belief by changing your words today!

WINNING ACTION!

Create your 'I am' Statements today and start to say them each day with Authority, with Visualization, and with Imagination!

(Create three I am statement about yourself. These are things that you believe you are or will be. These are three great things about you and your strengths.)

I am...

_____

I am...

_____

I am...

_____

WINNING CONFESSION!

I choose to speak ONLY positive things about myself and my career as an athlete. I will build my faith each day by believing for great things and speaking those things into existence. I choose not to accept negative talk about me or my career. I am a leader and a positive role model for other athletes. I WILL Create the Winning Mindset! I am a WINNER!

A WINNING ATHLETE...

"I started to train with coach JC and The DSD team because I loved how much energy they brought out to the gym and I knew they pushed your body to your fullest potential so if I wanted to be the best I knew I had to train with the best!

My life as an athlete before I came to the DSD was soooo negative and I didn't really have the right mindset or gameplay as a successful athlete. I was never that passionate or positive before DSD.

I have noticed now that I am a role model and that I have potential in anything that I do! I have more positive thinking and a strong urge to go out and earn what I have worked so hard for. I can now do this while also having fun and always smiling!

The most motivational quote Coach JC told me and that has stuck with me and I live by everyday is, "Great athletes do everyday what good athletes do occasionally!" So never be that guy who is only working hard because a coach or someone is watching you. You have to bust your butt everyday no matter what the circumstances are!

I have truly learned that having the right mindset is the key to success either on the field or in life! Staying positive and believing in your ability to do anything you want to. They say any game is 90% mental and only 10% physical so if you go into a game dreading it or scared before it even started the other team has you beat! Be positive and tell yourself your going to go out there and win!

Staying focused and committed to yourself! You can never take days off because I remember when coach said that when your taking days off your competition is getting better and putting great work in! So if you want to be the best go to your workouts at 5 in the morning and who knows maybe your completion is sleeping? Always put in your fullest effort in whatever you do!

Because a day wasted you will never get back! Never end the day asking or telling yourself, man only of I did one more or if I ran that extra sprint because "if you want something you've never had, you have to do something you've never done."

– Tyler Ellman, Airforce

CHAPTER TWENTY SIX

DIG DEEP

"Are you willing to sacrifice what you want at the moment for what you want most in life?"

– Coach JC

HOW BADLY DO YOU REALLY WANT IT?

How badly do you really want to have success as an athlete? How badly do you really want to play in the MLB? How badly do you really want to play in the NFL? Well, I have great news for you. Now you can; now is your time! You may be saying to yourself, "It is just not that simple coach." Of course it is. All it takes is one choice. Just one decision – made by you!

As you probably realize, much of life is a routine, and I have seen a lot of athletes become stale and stagnant. If you are not careful, it is very easy to fall into the trap of complacency. Make a decision starting today that you are not going to live another day on cruise control. Make a decision today that you are not going to allow your life to become stagnant. Have some passion about who you are, and make the decision to be passionate about what you are doing. It's your choice! Yes, it is that simple.

So many people allow others to make decisions for them on a daily basis; they allow people to choose their future for them. Not me and not you! You may not be the best on the team right now, you may not have the skills just yet, you may not live in the perfect environment, but remember, you can still choose to change any of that. It is just a choice, just one decision! Today, you are choosing to take control of your life by taking control of your THINKING. Today, you are choosing to take control of your life by taking control of your ATTITUDE. You choose your ACTIONS. You choose your RESULTS. You choose what your life looks like. You choose how much money you make. You choose what religion you practice. You choose what kind of marriage you have. You choose just about everything that happens on a daily basis. You choose who you are. It's YOUR choice!

Starting today, I want you to make a decision. Make the decision that your life is valuable and that you are worth it. You are done thinking about it! Starting today, you will no longer make excuses, and you will no longer accept anything else but GREATNESS. You will no longer accept anything but results! Start to make some big choices that are going to lead to big results. You MUST make a decision, a choice, to create an opportunity in your life that you may not have had otherwise.

WINNING ACTION!

What choice will I make today that will take me closer to my goal?

_____

_____

What choice will I make today that I will do every day to get me closer to my goal?

_____

_____

In what area of my life do I need to "Dig Deep" in order to achieve more?

_____

_____

WINNING CONFESSION!

Starting today, I make the decision that my life is valuable and that I am worth it. I will no longer make excuses, and I will no longer accept anything else but GREATNESS. I will no longer accept anything but results! Starting today I choose to make big choices that are going to lead to big results. I choose to make a decision, a choice, to create an opportunity in my life so that I can be a great athlete. I WILL Create the Winning Mindset! I am a WINNER!

A WINNING ATHLETE...

"I started training with Coach JC at DSD in order to prepare for the college level. I wanted to be prepared in every way I could, so I could focus on the soccer part of the game when I arrived. I wanted to know that every other aspect -- fitness, strength, agility, etc. -- was already above average. Prior to training at DSD, I could not play to my full potential multiple games in a row because my legs would tire due to fatigue and weakness. Also, I would constantly get knocked off of the ball because of my lack of upper body strength. I became a much more well-rounded individual strength wise. My legs were toned up and my arms just gained muscle. Because of Coach JC's program at DSD, when I left for college I was beyond prepared. I can now be confident in everything I am doing because I know I was physically and mentally prepared to take on whatever challenges are set against me. Mentally, I believe the greatest asset of training was the experience of accomplishment. Whether it was thinking I couldn't squat a certain amount of weight or do those last few prowlers, but then finishing whatever it may be, and being expected to do it to my full potential was that feeling that I learned. Once I experienced this feeling, I would constantly want it over and over again. I learned that that feeling was the one I needed to further even more in order to push myself to the next level."

– Katie Sprouse, Collegiate Soccer Athlete

CHAPTER TWENTY SEVEN

JUST DO IT

"Do it, and then you will feel motivated to do it."

- Zig Ziglar

NOW IT IS YOUR TIME!

You have learned over the last 26 chapters how to transform your thinking, take massive action each day, and have anything you want any time you want it as an athlete.

This chapter's short and sweet, my friend. You have everything you need to be successful. There is just one more thing left... JUST DO IT! Like our friends at Nike say, JUST DO IT!

It's simple. It really is... if you just do it! All you need to do is stay focused on the end result and do your one, simple, disciplined thing each day.

This chapter's short and sweet, my friend. You have everything you need to be successful. There is just one more thing left... JUST DO IT! Like our friends at Nike say, JUST DO IT!

It's simple. It really is... if you just do it! All you need to do is stay focused on the end result and do your one, simple, disciplined thing each day.

I want you now to commit to not just doing it, but to doing it in the best way that you possibly can. No more average! No more mediocre! So many people do things half-heartedly and just cruise through life. I am telling you that what you put into it is what you will get out it. It goes back to how badly do you want this? I want you to really think about this: in just 27 days, your life can be different! In just 27 days, you could be on your way to ultimate success as an athlete! In just 27 days, you can have The Winning Mindset to compete at the highest level!

In just 27 days you can create more focus, discipline, and confidence in your life! IN JUST 27 DAYS, my friend! Can you give it everything that you've got? Can you not just do it, but do it like there is no tomorrow? Is your life worth it? Is your career worth it? Actions speak louder than words: Show me what you've got! Just Do It!!!

WINNING ACTION!

Today I want you to go back to page one and start to refine all your daily actions steps for the next 27 days. Know your "WHAT", know your "WHY", know your Game Plan, and know your Daily Action Steps that will take you there.

WINNING CONFESSION!

I have been created with a purpose! I am not moved by what I feel or circumstances that happen. I WILL take purposeful action to get what I desire.

I am enthusiastic about being my best. I will maximize the moment. I will be a great student of the game.

I am a go-getter. I take massive action and always control my emotions and actions.

I choose today and each and every day to have a WINNER'S attitude. My attitude starting today will line up with what I desire. I will no longer allow my feelings and situations to determine my attitude for me.

Starting today, I make the decision that my life is valuable and that I am worth it. I will no longer make excuses, and I will no longer accept anything but GREATNESS. I will no longer accept anything but results! Starting today I choose to make big choices that are going to lead to big results. I choose to make a decision, a choice, to create an opportunity in my life so that I can be a great athlete.

Starting today I WILL expect more out of myself. I am not average, and I don't think like an average person. I am not mediocre, and I don't do mediocre things. I walk in excellence in ALL I do. In my personal life, in my relationships, and as an athlete, I set myself up for success by THINKING BIG!

I will stay focused and motivated on the end result and approach each day with no regret. I am grateful that the past is the past and I can start new today! I find ways on a daily basis to make it happen. It's now or never, and I choose to maximize the moment! I will stay focused and attack each day as I am on a mission to fulfill what I know I was called to do on this earth.

Starting today I choose to become accountable to myself and to others. I don't search for the easy way, but rather, I choose to take purposeful action even when I don't feel like it. I choose to just do it!

I choose to get back in the race. I am not a quitter and I choose to not quit. I will live today as if it were my last and enjoy every moment. I choose to create fun in my life and run my race.

I choose to speak ONLY positive things about myself and my career as an athlete. I will build my faith each day by believing for great things and speaking those things into existence. I choose not to accept negative talk about me or my career. I am a leader and a positive role model for other athletes. I WILL Create the Winning Mindset! I am a WINNER!

A WINNING ATHLETE...

CREATE YOUR WINNING STORY.

Today I want for you to create your winning story. You have now heard the success stories of over 26 athletes that I have been blessed and privileged to train and help WIN as an athlete and WIN in life. There are hundreds more and I want you to know that these athletes are no different than you. They just took this game plan and implemented it.

Now it's your turn!

Today you will create your future winning success story. Today I want for you to write down your testimony. I want for you to create your winning success story. This will be your success story. How you would think, act and feel once you have the success you are wanting as an athlete and in life. I want for you to write this like you are writing it to be in my next book. Write it from the perspective of you already have that success that you will have.

Have fun and WIN!

CONGRATULATIONS!

You did it! You completed your 27-day game plan so that you can have anything you want anytime that you want it in business and in life.

The principles that you have just read are simple, and they work if you just work them. Once you transform your thinking, you will be able to have that thing or things that you so badly desire.

THE CHOICE IS YOURS, MY FRIEND!

Remember, success is not some big event that just happens. It comes down to you executing your daily action steps and exercising the law of compound in your life. No one else can do it for you. Time can work for you or against you! What's your choice? How badly do you want this success?

I believe in you and know that you desperately want it. Listen to me, don't get overwhelmed, just follow the game plan and execute that one simple, disciplined thing every day that will get you to the promise land!

SO, WHERE DO YOU GO FROM HERE?

You go back to page one of this book and you go through every day again to assure that you are executing the game plan. Remember, retention without implementation is useless... What are you going to do with it?

YOU WERE BORN A WINNER.
WIN ALL DAY!

Coach JC

REQUEST COACH JC FOR YOUR NEXT EVENT

For over 17 years now Coach JC has been motivating individuals and organizations to to WIN in sport and in life!

It's time for you to WIN and WIN ALL DAY

I WOULD LOVE TO HEAR FROM YOU!

I know this book has changed your life! I would love to hear from you. Please write to me as I would love to hear how it has touched your life.

Contact me! Send letters to:
Coach JC
JJC Enterprises
8177 S Harvard Ave.
Suite 420
Tulsa, OK 74137

email or call us:
1 800-382-1506
email: jc@coachjc.com
website: www.CoachJC.com

Scan with a smartphone to connect with me on Facebook, Twitter & Instagram

ABOUT THE AUTHOR

COACH JC, YOUR LIFE SUCCESS COACH

coaches people on a daily basis on how to increase your winning percentage and WIN IN LIFE. As a Lifestyle, Fitness and Strength Coach, Coach JC's No Nonsense, No Excuse approach has been transforming lives for over 17 years now.

As an established Author, Speaker, and Coach he is regarded as one of the top Coaches in the entire country. He has been assisting individuals from all walks of life to "Take it to the next level!" Coach JC motivates people to take control of their life. Coach JC has a passion for helping people live the life they were born to live.

He is the Founder and President of JJC Enterprises, Life Coaching. He is the Founder of the well-recognized Sports Performance Company, Dynamic Sports Development, and the Founder of Bootcamp Tulsa, Tulsa's first ever, outdoor fitness program. Bootcamp Tulsa has been named one of the country's Top 10 Outdoor Fitness Bootcamps.

In addition, Coach JC is the Director of Strength and Conditioning at an NCAA Division I institution and the Creator of The Secret To REAL Weight Loss Success...FOR CHRISTIANS. Coach JC's coaching philosophy remains consistent in that he is dedicated to providing the tools necessary to empower individuals to create Ultimate Lifestyle Changes.

Coach JC's qualifications include a Bachelors of Science degree, a Life Coach certification, multiple coaching, sports performance and fitness certifications, with none more valuable than his 17 years in the trenches. He is the author of The WIN ALL DAY book series. He has also been a consultant to professional athletes, corporations, pageant contestants, businessmen, entrepreneurs, pastors, and others just like you.

Coach JC also inspires and coaches young entrepreneurs on how to follow their dreams and turn their passions into profits! He shows people how they can profit doing what they love to do, run their businesses with integrity, and make money at the same time!

WIN ALL DAY AT

www.CoachJC.com

WIN ALL DAY BOOK SERIES

Learn how to :

- Create your purpose driven, highly profitable brand.
- Create the winning mindset to achieve ulitmate success in life.
- Look, feel and perform your best with a 27 day gameplan.
- Create the winning mindset to win as an athlete and win in life.

GET YOURS TODAY AT WWW.COACHJC.COM